Cambridge Elements ☰

Elements in Theatre, Performance and the Political
edited by
Trish Reid
University of Reading
Liz Tomlin
University of Glasgow

THEATRES OF AUTOFICTION

Lianna Mark
LMU Munich

Shaftesbury Road, Cambridge CB2 8EA, United Kingdom

One Liberty Plaza, 20th Floor, New York, NY 10006, USA

477 Williamstown Road, Port Melbourne, VIC 3207, Australia

314–321, 3rd Floor, Plot 3, Splendor Forum, Jasola District Centre,
New Delhi – 110025, India

103 Penang Road, #05–06/07, Visioncrest Commercial, Singapore 238467

Cambridge University Press is part of Cambridge University Press & Assessment,
a department of the University of Cambridge.

We share the University's mission to contribute to society through the pursuit of
education, learning and research at the highest international levels of excellence.

www.cambridge.org
Information on this title: www.cambridge.org/9781009565363

DOI: 10.1017/9781009406970

First published 2024

A catalogue record for this publication is available from the British Library

ISBN 978-1-009-56536-3 Hardback
ISBN 978-1-009-40695-6 Paperback
ISSN 2753-1244 (online)
ISSN 2753-1236 (print)

Theatres of Autofiction

Elements in Theatre, Performance and the Political

DOI: 10.1017/9781009406970
First published online: October 2024

Lianna Mark
LMU Munich

Author for correspondence: Lianna Mark, l.n.mark@vu.nl

Abstract: This Element is the first monograph to focus on the presence and popularity in contemporary theatre of autofiction, a mode characterised by its mixture of autobiographical and fictional materials and generally associated with the cutting edge of literary fiction. To do so, it brings frameworks from literary and theatre studies to bear on a recent upsurge in plays that explicitly mobilise lived experience and its fictionalisation to political ends. Considering a comparative corpus of state-subsidised productions in Britain and Europe since the mid-2010s – both adaptations of literary works and plays written for the stage – this Element attends to autofiction's aesthetics and politics through its negotiation on stage of three conceptual binaries, each the focus of a chapter: fact/fiction, self/other, and inclusion/exclusion. By probing the mode's critical potential and pitfalls, it sheds light on the stakes of self-fictionalising practices in today's cultural markets and on the role of theatre therein.

Keywords: autofiction, theatre, authenticity, political, lived experience

ISBNs: 9781009565363 (HB), 9781009406956 (PB), 9781009406970 (OC)
ISSNs: 2753-1244 (online), 2753-1236 (print)

Contents

1 Introduction

In the first scene of Ella Hickson's *The Writer* (2018), commissioned by the Almeida Theatre in London, a young woman communicates her exasperation with contemporary theatre's stale repertoires to a theatre director. 'With Trump in, with the monstrosities going down, the world is cracking open', and yet all one finds on stage are 'famous people doing boring things badly' and '[r]eal-life babies. Like that's the only pulse we can find' (Hickson, 2018: 14–15). Discussing her involvement in the adaptation of Didier Eribon's *Returning to Reims*, produced in 2017 by Berlin's Schaubühne, the Manchester International Festival, Manchester's HOME, and Paris's Théâtre de la Ville, actor Nina Hoss explains the reasons behind her choice of a sociological memoir as dictated by similar considerations. Hoss recounts having turned down artistic director Thomas Ostermeier's initial proposal to adapt a monologue by Jean Cocteau: 'It interested me – I hadn't done a monologue – but after my experience in New York, and the aftermath of Trump's election, I thought, For now, I can't do this' (Zarin, 2018).

Both women use the then president of the United States Donald Trump as shorthand for the crises of our times, which are offered up, on and off stage, as proof of the insufficiency of made-up stories. And indeed, despite their high degree of fictionality, both plays are rooted explicitly in the real. Reaching beyond what writer Rachel Cusk has described as the 'fake and embarrassing' conventions of fiction – 'the idea of making up John and Jane and having them do things together' (Kellaway, 2014) – they engage in a search for forms that feel better suited to facing rather than evading reality today.

Neither production, however, is straightforwardly autobiographical. Rather, they tap into the autofictional: a mode that, despite being considered by many 'the hottest literary trend of the last decade' (Folarin, 2020), is yet to be systematically documented in the theatre. With its playful relationship to truth, its oscillatory movements between lived experience and fictionalisation, and its radically subjective stance, autofiction is – to speak with the fictional director in Hickson's play (21) – 'zeitgeisty' in more ways than one.

This Element explores the presence of the autofictional in contemporary theatre, offering a pragmatically oriented investigation of this mode and its political affordances on stage since the 2010s. In a 'post-truth' communication economy, in which the personal is relegated to echo chambers, mobilised in culture wars, or exploited – to quote Hickson's fictional director again – to 'get bums on seats' (21), frameworks that illuminate the aesthetics and politics of how lived experience is capitalised on, fictionalised, and performed in the public arena gain new and heightened resonance.

1.1 Autofiction from Page to Stage

From Karl-Ove Knausgaard to Annie Ernaux via Ben Lerner and Rachel Cusk, many of today's most successful writers have, to borrow a *Guardian* headline, 'stopped making things up' (Clark, 2018) – or rather, stopped making them up entirely. Revivifying the much-debated label first used by French writer Serge Doubrovsky on the back cover of his novel *Fils* (1977), they have instead been trading increasingly in 'fiction, of facts and events strictly real' (Doubrovsky, 2013: 1). Spurring this kind of experimentation is the intention to transcend the sedimented conventions of novel-writing, seen as inadequate to our times – residues of a dated, bourgeois, and/or androcentric worldview – and cease to dissimulate fiction's roots in the self and in the real.

Autofiction's origin story begins in France and, despite competition from Scandinavia and genealogical hunts for proto-autofiction throughout literary history (see Effe & Lawlor, 2022), the category has not entirely shed its French connotations, particularly in the Anglophone world. The term is often dismissed as 'more commonly used in French-language studies of autobiographical works' (Stephenson, 2013: 174) and, as Hywel Dix (2018: 7) bemoans, 'the number of Anglophone writers to have been explicitly identified as practitioners of the genre is comparably low'. While I am convinced these statements do not reflect the actual presence or popularity of autofictional work in Anglophone cultural markets, not least when looking beyond the printed page, they speak to a certain recalcitrance in acknowledging and thinking with the term beyond a small selection of novels.

There is little scholarship in general, and almost no Anglophone scholarship, on autofiction in the theatre,[1] aside from the occasional mention of the term or article defining a specific work or body of works as autofictional (e.g., Angel-Perez, 2013, 2016). In her study of Canadian drama, *Performing Autobiography*, Jennifer Stephenson (2013: 8) acknowledges that one of her case studies should be considered '"autofiction" rather than autobiography, recognizing the clearly fictional treatment of real-life situations and events in the playwright's life', then proceeds to dismiss the term's 'French' specificity. Deirdre Heddon does something similar in *Autobiography and Performance* (Heddon, 2008: 13), while also registering a broader tendency to mix fact and fiction in several of the works discussed (47, 50) or to foreground 'the gap between the self that is being narrated and the self that is performing' (46). In line with many autobiography scholars who dismiss the category of autofiction tout court, considering it inseparable from the autobiographical (e.g., Smith & Watson, 2001: 186), Heddon ultimately

---

[1] Transmedial autofiction scholarship tends to focus on film, self-portrait, photography, etc. (e.g., Dix, 2018; Wagner-Egelhaaf, 2019; Effe & Lawlor, 2022).

includes these possibilities within the latter's remit, and autofictional performance is given no specific attention. A French-language edited collection (Fix and Toudoire-Surlapierre, 2011) chooses to tackle the issue of autofictionality in contemporary theatre – among a range of other types of so-called 'autofiguration' – through a broad selection of case studies from Tadeusz Kantor to Sarah Kane, focusing on theoretical debates and textual analysis of what are identified as the mode's intrinsic properties. Finally, early steps towards initiating a conversation on theatre and autofiction in the Anglophone world are made in my own previous writing on the topic (Mark, 2023). This Element is written in the hope of further filling this lacuna.

Turning from scholarship to the theatre industry, the difference in the currency of the term 'autofiction' in the UK compared to continental Europe gains sharp relief. In Europe, it is deployed with increasing frequency in marketing and critical reception: without explanations, it is used and received as indicating the staged equivalent of literary autofiction. Berlin's Schaubühne and Maxim Gorki Theater, for instance, describe a range of productions as 'autofictional' on their websites: not only the adaptations of literary works of autofiction by Annie Ernaux and Édouard Louis, but also plays by Falk Richter and Angélica Liddell – the success of the former type facilitating the latter's proliferation. In the British theatre industry, on the other hand, the term is effectively absent. Perhaps signalling an incipient change, a notable exception is British playwright Alexander Zeldin's *The Confessions* (2023), based on his mother's life, which was, however, co-produced by eleven international institutions[2] and is touring Europe at the time of writing. In an interview for the *Guardian*, Zeldin describes the play as an attempt to 'do' autofictional theatre, inspired by Ernaux and Cusk: 'I wanted to try to write something that I didn't have a model for in theatre, but was there in their novels. [...] I feel the novel has found a way for the writing of that self that the theatre hasn't in the same way' (Crompton, 2023).

While autofiction on stage exists, then – even simply on account of the term's industry circulation, and of the incremental adaptations of literary works labelled as such – it defies straightforward definition, perhaps even more than on the page. Given the mode's hybrid conceptualisation (part autobiography, part fiction), and its context-dependent, interactive qualities that are only augmented in the theatre, micro-definitory efforts in the abstract have obvious limitations, as illustrated by the 'Autofiction' entry in Patrice Pavis's *Routledge Dictionary of Performance and Contemporary Theatre* (Pavis, 2016: 22–24). Pavis distinguishes between

---

[2] Wiener Festwochen, Comédie de Genève, Odéon-Théâtre de l'Europe, Centro Cultural de Belém, Théâtre de Liège, Festival d'Avignon, Festival d'Automne à Paris, Athens Epidaurus Festival, Piccolo Teatro di Milano – Teatro d'Europa, Adelaide Festival, and Centre Dramatique National de Normandie-Rouen.

'theatrical autofiction' and 'autoperformance',[3] justifying the former's rareness with the unexplained requirements of 'dramatization, transposition and the reprise of autobiographical elements from the author's life, elements reconstituted in their unprocessed form into stage actions' (23). Without addressing the issue of how anything on stage might be 'unprocessed', the rationale behind the listed requirements, nor the 'huge demands on the time and patience of the audience' he claims they would make, Pavis concludes that 'every autoperformance is just an autofiction' (23), collapsing the previously staked distinctions and leaving little to work with for analytic purposes.

Adding to the challenge of defining autofiction is the mode's significant overlap with the autobiographical,[4] which is further heightened on stage. There are many reasons for this overlap. Most obviously, the illusion of 'objective telling' is even less attainable in the iterative, embodied medium of theatre, not least due to the presence of an actor/performer[5] pretending. Indeed, as every play involves some degree of fictionality, most instances of autobiographical performance fit within the framework of autofiction (see Leroux, 2004: 75). That said, while most autobiographical performances[6] could be considered (somewhat) autofictional, many plays that work autofictionally are – as we shall see – clearly not autobiographical. The two categories, then, overlap but do not correspond, with the autofictional comprising a set of practices that complicate and push back against the tendency to engage with the autobiographical in a 'treasure hunt for the "real"' (Clark, 2018).

Without the ambition of providing its own definition of autofictional theatre in absolute terms nor staking a claim to the mode's radical novelty, this Element attends to a recent, international upsurge in plays that work autofictionally. By this I mean dramatic works based on a script with (a) clearly identifiable author(s) – either written for the stage or adapted from literary works – that draw explicitly on the lived experience of the author(s) and, crucially, are marketed as (somewhat) authentic. Alongside real source material, they highlight their own fictionalisation,

---

[3] 'When what is said of the self is simultaneously embodied or shown by an actor (a performer), we call it 'self-performance' (*autoperformance*). In this case, actors can become performers. Performers claim that they are just being themselves, that they are not representing a character but speaking directly of their own lives: they have exchanged representation for the presentation of self' (Pavis, 2016: 21).

[4] Since Doubrovsky (2013: 3) qualified autofiction as a 'postmodern version of autobiography', much ink has been spilled on whether, how, and to what extent it differs from kindred modes or genres including autobiography, memoir, life writing, and autotheory.

[5] See footnote 3.

[6] And indeed, a great deal of performance art, in which many of the features I identify in the following chapters are well established (see, e.g., the work of Spalding Gray). This Element, however, explores these features from the vantage point of text-based theatre, establishing their currency in a different tradition to performance/body/live art and in association with the questions and struggles of transmedial autofiction.

often by including the narration or enactment of experiences that cannot be or do not come across as real. In line with literary autofiction, they also feature moments of meta-narrative and/or metatheatrical reflection, foregrounding 'the process of invention in self-narration, or the discursive construction of the self' (Srikanth, 2019: 348; see also Weigel, 2011: 26). Finally, their displayed interest in the role of narrative in constructing individual and social identities tends to be harnessed to social justice struggles, making manifest some form of political engagement.

While acknowledging significant overlaps with autobiographical performance, then, it is my belief that the currency of the autofictional in the cultural marketplace, the runaway popularity of stage adaptations of literary autofiction, and the frequency of the characteristics listed in the previous paragraph featuring together in theatre productions since the mid-2010s warrant a discussion of how theatre might function autofictionally; what it can contribute to the conversation on autofiction; and what the lens of autofictionality on stage might make visible within the realm of autobiographical performance and of self-storytelling practices at large. This approach circumvents the problem, outlined by Heddon (2008: 9–10), of establishing whether a production that draws on (what appears to be) autobiographical material, but does not declare itself as such, is effectively autobiographical. Indeed, regardless of what the play or performance *is*, it can be seen, given certain conditions, to *function* autofictionally.[7] Vice versa, the autofictional can be understood as 'an intrinsic mode within the autobiographical that can be performed in various ways and with changing intensity' (Wagner-Egelhaaf, 2022: 24). By considering these ways and intensities, this Element aims in no way to write against autobiography scholarship. Rather, to borrow Heddon's phrase, it hopes to stage another possible 'encounter with a broader practice' (Heddon, 2008: 12), from a different perspective and embedded in different contexts.

In demarcating this Element's object of study, I extend a pragmatic understanding of the term 'autofiction' across media, in the hope that the insights gained will not only justify but also feed back into the porous identification criteria provided. Crucially, I hope to encourage the acknowledgement of a broader and more diverse range of theatrical works *as* autofictional or as *working* autofictionally, attending to what they share across cultural contexts and to the political affordances of the mode's deployment on stage. As Arianne Zwartjes (2019) points out, gathering works under a label – without losing sight of the fluid and somewhat arbitrary nature thereof – 'allows us to think about and probe the edges of that category, its functions and its politics, what new things it might offer us', as well as 'to *find*' a work in the first place, 'and to examine it alongside other conceptually-similar work' (emphasis original).

---

[7] See footnote 32.

The act itself of 'finding' a work of autofiction has particularly high stakes when it comes to cultural politics as it substantially alters the value systems into which a work is received. As writer Tope Folarin puts it, '[a]utofiction is at the cutting edge of literary innovation; autobiographical fiction is as old as time. When a critic invokes the phrase "autofiction" they are essentially arguing that a writer is helping to create a new kind of literature. The phrase "autobiographical fiction," on the other hand, denotes a book that could very well be artful but is drawing on a tradition that isn't new at all'. This maps onto the homogeneity of the autofictional canon, populated largely by the work of white, bourgeois writers from the Global North credited with refracting universal aspects of contemporary subjectivity through experimental manipulation of narrative form. Conversely, marginalised writers fictionalising aspects of their own experience are often relegated to the sphere of autobiographical fiction, their lives seen not merely as informing but as taking precedence over their art (see Folarin, 2020). Their art is thus often reduced, in reception, to a documentation of lived experiences of marginalisation, with the purpose of conveying – as novelist Brandon Taylor (2021) ironically documents, in the context of 'black art' – 'what it means to contend *blackly* with the *black* imponderables and the unruly *black* quandaries of *black* life' (emphasis original), where 'black' can be replaced by whichever form of marginalisation applies.

It is perhaps unsurprising, then, that among the plays in the corpus only those by white playwrights (e.g., *The Confessions*, *The Silence*) are explicitly referred to as autofictional. Undergirding this is a broader industry dynamic whereby marginalised artists are often 'given voice' – as the awkward expression has it – on condition that they speak from within and about their experiences of marginalisation, to the point that 'authenticity' and 'diversity' have become de facto synonyms in the industry (see Goodling & Mark, 2022).

In this context, importing the framework of autofictionality from literary studies can elicit a recognition of authorial agency and critical potential – whether delivered upon or not – within and beyond the fetishisation of the author/performer's 'authentic voice' (Beswick, 2014). It can foreground the aesthetic and meta-narrative qualities of the work, which, though far from a prerogative of autofiction, can easily be dethroned in criticism and reception of material received as authentic in favour of 'a prurient, limiting conflation' of the story told with the writer's life (Satin & Jerome, 1999: 12). In short, it can encourage the spectator/reader to look beyond 'the inevitable prevalence of the self' and focus, instead, 'on the particularities of self-construction' in the narration of lived experience (Gibbons, 2017: 117).

This Element's approach is shaped by these considerations, understanding the autofictional not as an intrinsic property of a work but as a mode of reading or receiving (aspects of) it.[8] Stories can thus gain or shed autofictionality as they travel across media and locales, depending on the ever-changing relationship between the text (in the broadest sense), its (marketing and editorial) paratexts,[9] and its (material and discursive) contexts, just as a book's genre today depends on editorial metadata, on what is written on the cover, on which display table it is placed on in a bookstore, and on what is made public about the author and how. In doing so, I follow a recent scholarly move away from autofiction as a genre towards 'the autofictional' as a 'mode, moment, and strategy that can appear in a variety of texts across time' (Effe & Lawlor, 2022: 4): 'an inherent dimension of autobiographical writing'; 'a latent force that can be activated in different ways and to different degrees'; and – crucially for theatre – a 'conceptual matrix with scalable and interactive dimensions' (Wagner-Egelhaaf, 2022: 23–26). It is an understanding of the autofictional as local, relational, and context-dependent that this Element's title aims to emphasise, in highlighting not autofictional plays as a dramatic genre but specific, time-limited, localisable *theatres of autofiction*.

While the following sections will delve into the institutional and cultural contexts of individual productions, significant shifts in mediatised communication and cultural market dynamics undergird this Element's corpus as a whole, shaped in turn by a range of structural changes to our economic system. Indeed, as our systems of production and distribution strive to 'cut out the middleman', making all interactions and transactions as unmediated and continuous as possible, they have engendered a culture style based on immediacy, transparency, and authenticity (see Kornbluh, 2023), but also – I would add – in its more critical manifestations, increasingly preoccupied with the questioning of these ubiquitous qualities. Far from constituting a sealed-off arena of social critique, the aesthetics, narrative structures, and dramaturgies of the autofictional are thus part and parcel of a broader turn to apparently intimate self-storytelling that blends authentic lived experience with standardised scripts; draws attention to the person behind the product; and participates in a post-truth enchantment with the affective power of fictionalisation, as the next section explores.

---

[8] See Effe & Lawlor, 2022: 4; Ferreira-Meyers, 2018: 41.

[9] By 'paratext' I mean the content designed to present and comment on the play (including interviews, promotional materials, etc.), whereas 'contexts' include any material conditions and discursive formations that inform or interact with but are not designed for the play. For Gérard Genette (1997: 1–2), a paratext is a 'threshold' or, 'as Philippe Lejeune put it, "a fringe of the printed text which in reality controls one's whole reading of the text." Indeed, this fringe, always the conveyor of a commentary that is authorial or more or less legitimated by the author, constitutes a zone between text and off-text, a zone not only of transition but also of transaction: a privileged place of a pragmatics and a strategy, of an influence on the public'. In today's cultural marketplace, paratextual commentary is rarely 'authorial' and more often curated by others.

1.2 Everybody Has a Story

Recent years have seen spectacular successes for self-narration under various guises. First Annie Ernaux, widely known as the 'grande dame of autofiction', was awarded the 2022 Nobel Prize, followed by Norwegian autofiction writer Jon Fosse in 2023; then *Spare* (2023) – Prince Harry's ostensible attempt to 'own [his] story' (Lawless, 2023) – broke first-day sale records as the most successful nonfiction book ever published by the world's largest publisher Penguin Random House (see Alter & Harris, 2023). Ernaux and Prince Harry are not the kind of writers whose work tends to lie side by side on a bookstore display table. Yet their twinned successes have something to say about the broader context in which autofictional works are received and consumed, at a time when, as Heddon (2008: 7) argues, the personal is increasingly valued as 'a popular and cheaply manufactured commodity'.

The 'cheap manufacturing' of the personal identified by Heddon plays a role in several interconnected spheres; I will touch briefly on the four most relevant to autofiction. First, the advent of the internet with its social-mediatised[10] discourse has created an unprecedented range of platforms for direct and apparently intimate self-storytelling, in which truth becomes a radically subjective matter, to be vouched for through media-specific, authenticity-simulating conventions (see Georgakopoulou, 2022). This rebranding of truth as 'personal' has percolated into political debate, increasingly relegated to the sphere of symbolic posturing, and capitalised on by online platforms as an aggression-fuelled, addictive hook serving to maximise user engagement. Incidentally, the extent and effect of these changes are encapsulated in two semantic drifts: 'engagement' today evokes not Sartrian political commitment but a measure of audience interaction with content; while a 'call to action' (CTA) is not principally an incitement to activist politics but a way of interactively fostering user engagement online (see Georgakopoulou, 2022). A mode harnessing lived experience to political struggles by performing authenticity and playing with forms of truth beyond the merely factual thus has evident timeliness, but also risks reproducing the empty gestures of online positioning. Fittingly, many scholars and cultural critics see autofiction as one of the 'dominant narrative forms of the selfie-generation' (Iversen, 2020: 560; see also Worthen, 2021). In Stefan Iversen's words, the mode's 'radical individualisation, its focus on affects, the actualization of trans- and intermedial storytelling practices, the revelatory nature of extreme confessions – all these factors render autofiction ideally suited for a post-social media landscape' (Iversen, 2020: 560).

---

[10] Unlike 'mediation', the term 'mediatisation' indicates processes that reflexively link communication to commoditization (see Jaffe, 2011).

Second, and relatedly, the takeover of publishing on the part of multinational conglomerates and media corporations has augmented the value of the 'auto' in autofiction. This is linked to a privileging of easy marketability, guaranteed by the 'attractive and articulate real people' behind the works, who can 'speak from the heart of the product' (Brouillette, 2020) and thereby capitalise on a widespread appetite for the authentic, the personal, and at its most extreme, the voyeuristic (so-called 'trauma porn') – highly valued currencies in today's cultural markets. Moreover, the promise of access to authentic individual experience – often of overcoming marginalisation or trauma, as vouched for by the writing itself – appeals to the forms of self-help culture thriving under neoliberal capitalism, as it 'intensifies and personalises the novel as therapy' (Brouillette, 2020): a how-to guide to individual survival.

These shifts in social-mediatised discourse, cultural production, and critical and popular reception feed into the rise of 'relatability' as a measure of value, which tends to reduce the empathetic and identificatory responses elicited by aesthetic experience to a matter of recognition predicated on sameness (see Mead, 2014; Thomson, 2018; Georgakopoulou, 2022). Indeed, the popularisation of formatted[11] scenarios in the second person – featured in memes and 'stories' on so-called 'egomedia' (i.e., TikTok, Instagram, etc.) and signalled, for example, by the captions 'tfw' ('that feeling when') or 'POV' ('point of view')[12] – has been recoding the logics of sharing through stories by inviting validation through relatability: this really did happen to you, in other words, *because* I have experienced something similar. An analogous dynamic can often be traced in the autofictional. Feeding into the so-called 'storification' of the social, the incremental reliance on these communicative formats, coupled with their formatting power, has been reshaping our consumption of stories in general and self-narrative practices in particular, as the plays in this study show. Against this backdrop, this Element's framework and analytic approach exceeds, in its relevance and applicability, the confines of theatre and performance.

Third, what is widely known as the 'post-truth' communication economy[13] has arguably heightened the appeal of autofiction's recognition of its own untruth and ambiguity (the 'fiction' in autofiction). With its explicit mix of

---

[11] Formatting indicates how 'certain types of stories and ways of telling them become recognizable, normative, and sought after on platformed environments' (Georgakopoulou, 2022: 267), thereby eliciting scripted responses. It means 'shaping the particular situated interaction in "typical" (i.e., generic, non-unique) ways' (Blommaert, Smits, & Yacoubi, 2020: 57).

[12] For example, 'TFW you realise your ex is now someone else's problem' or 'POV a tired millennial teacher at the end of the school year', accompanied by relevant comical images: in the first case, irrepressible glee, in the second, exhausted resignation.

[13] Chosen as Oxford Dictionaries' international word of the year in 2016, 'post-truth' is defined as 'relating to or denoting circumstances in which objective facts are less influential in shaping public opinion than appeals to emotion and personal belief' (*OED*).

truth and lies, autofiction both complements and contrasts a political discourse in which incompatible claims accumulate with no accountability or reckoning, while whatever is in the public sphere has a chance of being picked up, shared, and woven as further evidence into pre-existent narratives, regardless of its truth content. In contrast to this, a mode of storytelling ready to admit to its frank manipulation of reality comes across as paradoxically deserving of trust.

Finally, autofiction's ascent has been flanked by the so-called 'storytelling boom' (Mäkelä & Meretoja, 2022), or the incremental recourse to storytelling in a range of non-literary/artistic fields.[14] From managerial strategies via dating apps to funding applications and political spin, (self-)storytelling has become a ubiquitous discursive mode, serving to elicit receivers' sympathies, make ideas relatable, and vouch for the legitimacy of a communicative act. While the empathy-inspiring, therapeutic, inclusion-furthering, and imagination-unlocking properties of narrative are being touted by economists, health professionals, and communication consultants alike, the new valorisation of lived experience as a locus of unnegotiable truth comes often at the cost of more intersubjective hermeneutic frameworks (see Mäkelä & Meretoja, 2022).

Parsing 'good stories' and 'bad stories' as a way of squaring noble intentions with a compromised communication economy, however, has its limits. And indeed, these two phenomena – the runaway success of autofiction, and the boom in applied self-storytelling – are, I argue, not entirely separable; rather, like Ernaux and Prince Harry, they awkwardly occupy the same arena, tapping into kindred collective appetites to various and often incompatible ends. In their parallel developments, they have, in a sense, met in the middle. On the one hand, autofiction has shifted from the psychoanalytically informed experiments of 1970s France, focused on 'universal' experiences like language and memory, to the transmedial mode this Element identifies, rooted in lived experiences of marginalisation and invested in issue-based political struggles. Self-storytelling, on the other hand, has moved away from its roots in the political organising of feminist consciousness-raising groups of the 1960s and '70s and been progressively mainstreamed and co-opted, giving rise – as Sujatha Fernandes documents (Fernandes, 2017: 13) – to 'the transactional, therapeutic, and then market-based model [. . .] that currently dominates'.

By acknowledging the impact of these transformations on autofiction's critical reception, market success, and political affordances, this Element is alive to the role of 'storytelling within broader neoliberal transformations' (Fernandes, 2017: 10). In particular, it attends to the risk of storytelling

---

[14] For clarity, I distinguish between self-narration, i.e., artistic/literary practices, and applied 'self-storytelling'.

becoming complicit with 'the neoliberal doctrine that highlights the upward mobility of an individual, while downplaying supra-individual societal structures and processes' (Mäkelä & Meretoja, 2022: 192). This is heightened in narratives of victimhood, (previous or ongoing) marginalisation, and/or upward social mobility: increasingly common themes in autofictional works. As addressed in Section 4, similar storylines risk celebrating the resilient individual as proof that systemic oppression can and indeed should be overcome through talent and willpower, while leaving societal structures untouched.

Alongside the risk of co-option, the boom in self-storytelling has also brought forth, in spheres that have always dealt in stories, a heightened awareness of both the potential and pitfalls of self-narration. Much autofiction, I argue, emerges out of this awareness, responding with metafictional and/or metatheatrical reflection, avoidance of purely confessional registers, and critical engagement with the exploitation of lived experience in and by the creative industries.

1.3 Setting the Scene

Finally, a brief note on the geographical, cultural, and temporal remit of this Element. The plays in its corpus are all (co-)productions by British and/or German venues, at times in collaboration with other international institutions. To keep them commensurable and contextualised, I focus on productions by steadily state-funded institutions of comparable size and status. Due to my own location at the time of writing, these comprise works performed (also, but not exclusively) in London and Berlin: at London's Royal Court, Almeida Theatre, Battersea Arts Centre, National Theatre, and Bush Theatre; and at Berlin's Schaubühne and Berliner Ensemble.

As discussed in Section 1.1, the label of 'autofiction' has been attributed prevalently to the work of white authors from the Global North. While this Element is written with the intention of diversifying the corpus of works identified as autofictional, it remains constrained to British and European institutions and productions. This European focus reflects, on the one hand, the canonical history of the mode's development, and on the other, my own scholarly, cultural, and linguistic expertise and location. I write in the awareness, however, of a rich history of self-fictionalisation preceding Doubrovsky and spanning global cultures, in the hope that others might complement this story.

Despite these limitations, the comparison between British theatre and its idealised, European 'other' (see Stephens, 2012) offers several advantages. It allows the juxtaposition of different theatres of autofiction, embedded in their respective institutional and funding landscapes: on the one hand, plays advertised *as* autofictional and adaptations of literary autofiction, which have become a trend in European theatres; on the other, British productions whose autofictionality is yet to be recognised. The comparative approach, moreover, offers insights into the aesthetic and political projects of theatres of autofiction in both countries, which reflect, each in their own way, a culturally specific understanding of the role and responsibilities of state-subsidised theatre at large. Finally, while autofiction's story begins in France, Germany has played a crucial role in translating and adapting French autofiction for the stage. Starting in the mid-2010s, Berlin's Schaubühne was the first theatre to systematically adapt texts by Eribon, Louis, and Ernaux: three upwardly mobile writers and friends, hailing from working-class communities in Northern France, whose work is widely received as autofictional (Louis's and Ernaux's) or autotheoretical (Eribon's).[15] As these adaptations constitute the first widely acknowledged theatre of autofiction, it is with these that this Element begins. From there, it turns to the UK to identify a theatrical mode that, despite its popularity, has yet to find acknowledgement.

The plays I analyse premiered between 2015 and 2023, the latter limit corresponding to the time of writing. While the characteristics described can, of course, be found in plays predating 2015, beginning in the mid-2010s allows me to both consider a constellation of coeval works, anchored in the upsurge in adaptations of French autofiction, and reveal the mode's incremental presence and popularity.

Drawing on thirteen case studies and circling back to them throughout, *Theatres of Autofiction* sheds light on the popularity of a theatrical mode that fictionalises the personal to politicised ends, that is, with a focus on political subjectivation, processes of marginalisation, and resistance. Specifically, it explores how autofiction's political affordances take shape on stage in the negotiation of three binaries, each the focus of a section: fact/fiction, self/other, and inclusion/exclusion. Section 2 identifies and illustrates a range of authenticating devices and markers of fictionalisation, whose cooperation on stage signals the presence of the autofictional and complicates its promise of authenticity. To do so, it looks at *DenMarked* (2015), *salt.* (2016), *Returning to Reims* (2017 & 2021), *Misty* (2018), *Superhoe* (2019), *Who Killed My Father* (2020), *The Silence* (2023), and *Happening* (2023). With a range of brief examples (including *DenMarked* (2015), *salt.* (2016), *Refuge Woman* (2018), *Poet in da Corner* (2018), *Superhoe* (2019), *Who Killed My Father* (2020), *The Silence* (2023), *Happening* (2023) and *The Confessions* (2023)), followed by

---

[15] Or rather, seen as spearheading a sociologically motivated avant-garde within autofiction. While Eribon's work is considered autotheoretical (in the UK and US) or autosociobiographical (in Germany), its stage adaptations at the Schaubühne function autofictionally, as detailed in Section 4.

two, in-depth analyses (of *The Writer* (2018) and *History of Violence* (2018)), Section 3 considers how theatres of autofiction negotiate the representation of, and boundaries between, self and other: the former, a space of transpersonal identification; the latter, of difference and alterity. Finally, Section 4 investigates the performative dimension of autofiction in its blending of life and narrative. Considering the role of class in the works and their material contexts, with a focus first on adaptations of social mobility stories at the Schaubühne (*Returning to Reims* (2017 & 2021), *History of Violence* (2018) and *Who Killed My Father* (2020)) and then on their British counterparts (*DenMarked* (2015), *Refuge Woman* (2018) and *Poet in da Corner* (2018)), it parses the logics of inclusion and exclusion reflected on and enacted by the productions. As the autofictional is defined by transgression, of 'generic, textual, and moral boundaries' (Iversen, 2020: 559), transgressive play across these three conceptual binaries will guide this Element's reflections.

2 Fact/Fiction

Following a performance of Conrad Murray's play *DenMarked* (2015) at Tom Thumb Theatre in Margate, a post-show discussion, filmed and made available on the performer's website,[16] captures the ambivalence of the spectatorial experience of autofictionality. Performed by Murray, the one-man show – the title of which refers both to Hamlet's homeland and the fact of being marked by one's 'den' (slang for 'home') – mixes theatre and hip hop to reflect on Murray's experience of growing up in poverty. The Q&A is dominated by a visibly perturbed audience member, who is quick to pin Murray down vis-à-vis the piece's authenticity. 'Because it's ostensibly autobiographical', the spectator intervenes, interrupting Murray's attempt to address their previous question,

> I have to say that because I don't know it for a fact. [. . .] When I said it was ostensibly autobiographical, I couldn't tell whether this was dead straight or partly fictionalised or a composite or whatever. That authenticity is what really came across. It was real. [. . .] I was moved, but I was a bit wary because I couldn't be certain whether you could – could you really have been saying this about real people? Because – it must have been fictioned. And so that was the tension for me: that lack of knowledge. (Murray, 0:49-12:18. www.conradmurray.org/new-page)

The spectator is clear about what they found compelling: the material's authenticity, coupled with uncertainty and unease about its referential status, despite the production's marketing as autobiographical. They are responding, here, to the autofictionality at work in the text: indeed, the perceived oscillation

---

[16] www.conradmurray.org/new-page.

between fact and fiction is widely acknowledged as one of the mode's constitutive features. With reference to Philippe Lejeune's autobiographical pact (Lejeune, 1975), according to which the author is expected to tell nothing but the truth, Doubrovsky himself described his books as 'neither autobiographies nor entirely novels, caught in the turnstile between genres, subscribing at once and contradictorily to the autobiographical and the fictional pact' (Doubrovsky, 1993: 210, my translation). While some scholars reject the idea of a text being received as factual and fictional at once (see Schmitt, 2010), others conceptualise the two pacts as fundamental to the mode's success – which would depend on 'the unresolvable paradox of these contradictory reading instructions' (Zipfel, 2005: 36) – and as alternating rather than synchronous: 'a revolving door' that moves the reader continuously from one to the other (Wagner-Egelhaaf, 2022: 32). This metaphor captures the pacts' entanglement, making of autofiction less the negotiation of a binary than a Möbius strip uniting the two in fluid motion: 'a dynamic and versatile mental concept which alternately brings one or the other dimension into the foreground while still allowing the other to permanently resonate' (Wagner-Egelhaaf, 2022: 33).

This section examines the interplay between authenticating devices and markers of fictionalisation on stage. It shows how, in the 'revolving door' of fact/fiction, confessional self-narration is complicated as its political stakes take shape. By referring to the 'sites and signposts of fictionality or factuality' (James, 2022: 44) not as 'fact' and 'fiction' but as 'authenticating devices' and 'markers of fictionalisation', I intend to emphasise their constructed nature. Particularly in the time-limited experience of the theatregoer, factuality and fictionality are less discrete and verifiable dimensions of a production than the (somewhat subjective) effect of devices that 'foreground either referential force or the work of fictionalization' (42).

Like in literary autofiction, it is in the 'referential ground of the I' that 'sites of fictionalization' (56) are rooted in the theatre. This 'referential ground' (that is, the extent to which the 'I' is connected to a real person) is established with varying degrees of evidence either on stage or contextually, for example, in the production's marketing. Its extension and texture, as well as the degree and reach of the fictionalisation embedded therein – what James calls the 'relationship between global and local factuality and fictionality' (55) – vary greatly, ranging from works that claim to make nothing up and minimise markers of fictionalisation, to those that veer into the supernatural. The more the referential ground is insisted upon and the fictionalisation hidden or naturalised, the closer one is to the autobiographical; conversely, the more marked the fictionalisation, the more the autofictional shines through.

The negotiation of a performance's shifting referential status generates uncertainties, which may be playful or unsettling or both. Causing the spectator to question 'what interpretative and evaluative regimes appropriately apply' (Korthals Altes, 2014: 191) – as is visible in the *DenMarked* Q&A – these uncertainties elicit 'a meta-hermeneutic state of higher reflexiveness', which results in a rethinking of 'not only generic frames but more broadly frames of value generation and value ascription per se' (Iversen, 2020: 559). Indeed, empathetic response, ethical considerations, and expectations around original-ity, style, structure, and artfulness depend, in reception, on the referential status of what one is engaging with.

The spectator's questions to Murray exemplify the potential intensity of this 'meta-hermeneutic state'. It is their first intervention, however, that is most revealing. 'Well, that begs the question', they ask, 'could this work as well if it wasn't about you?' (Murray, 2019, 1:20–1:26. www.conradmurray.org/new-page). Not-so-subtly implied is a lack of craft in the performance, seen – considering the traumatic experiences grappled with – as merely confessional: a staged version of the 'autobiographical fiction' discussed in the Introduction, in which life takes precedence over art and authenticity replaces talent.

To shed light on the logics of the supply and demand of authenticity[17] in today's theatres of autofiction, and on the crucial role of fictionalisation in complicating this commerce, this section turns first to the use of authenticating devices, then to markers of fictionalisation on stage. It argues that understanding the autofictional as curated rather than confessional – or rather, as a curated performance *of* the confessional – illuminates its critical potential in contem-porary cultural markets.

2.1 Authenticating Devices

The curation of authenticity seals its paradoxical status as a contrived perform-ance of the uncontrived, evoked in the autofictional through 'signposts of factuality' (James, 2022: 52). In the theatre, these can be grouped into the three, overlapping categories explored in this section: people; objects, including props and other materials present on stage; and metatheatre, created at times through one or both of the former.

Authenticating people include the author of the source text, the playwright, and the performer(s);[18] they can authenticate with their name, their body, their voice, and/or their (public) biography. Akin to the literary, the most prominent

---

[17] For more on this, see Schulze, 2017.

[18] Potentially also the director, if their authorship over a production is central. The question of where the autofictional is located in different theatre traditions, and the competing influences of actors, directors, playwrights, etc., requires further study.

authenticating device on stage is 'the referential force [. . .] of the autodiegetic "I"' (James, 2022: 45), pronounced by (a) character(s). While much literary theory locates this referential force in the correspondence between the author's and the character's name, this pairing can be suggestively refracted and multiplied in theatres of autofiction. A range of scenarios are possible: one might find onomastic correspondence between the playwright, a(n)/the performer/actor, and a character; between the playwright or the author of an adaptation's source text and (one of) the character(s) on stage; and/or between the performer and their character (but, for example, not the playwright). Examples include Louis playing himself in an adaptation of his own text, *Who Killed My Father*; actor Dimitrij Schaad announcing matter-of-factly he will now 'become Falk Richter' in Richter's play *The Silence*; and actor Isabelle Redfern in the role of an actor called Isabelle in the second Schaubühne adaptation of *Returning to Reims*, adding her own autofictional lines to Eribon's text.

The primacy of the name in establishing the presence of the autofictional, however, is widely questioned. Drawing on Philippe Gasparini, Arnaud Schmitt (2022: 88) argues that '[a] stronger case can be made for labelling a text as autofiction when there is a certain resemblance between narrator and author based on similar biographical features than when the only conjunction is the name. Without these "identification operators," the name remains empty'. The same applies on stage. In the absence of onomastic correspondence, autofictionality might be suggested by similarities between the author (or a co-creator of the performance) and a character on several levels at once, including age, gender, class, ethnicity, idiolect, aspirations, and profession (see Schmitt, 2022: 88). Alternatively, the production might be marketed as autofictional, 'semi-autobiographical', or based on a true story. Without correspondence of names, then, the referential ground is established through textual (or performative), paratextual, and/or contextual indicators that encourage the assumption that one or more of the dramatis personae is a (version of a) real person involved in the production of the text or play.

Nicôle Lecky's play *Superhoe* (2019), produced at London's Royal Court Theatre and adapted into *Mood* (2022), a six-part TV series for BBC Three, is a choral example of authentication through people. At work in the text, performance, and paratext is a twofold, contradictory authentication, predicated at once on the playwright and on anonymous people she spoke to during the writing process, whose story the play is based on. On the one hand, playwright-performer (Lecky) and protagonist (Sasha) share a range of identification operators. Both are young women from East London of mixed British-Jamaican heritage. Both are singers: the production includes Sasha's songs, written and performed by Lecky. They share a sociolect, legible in the play's paratext: 'Thank you for your directing magic, girlllllll' and 'you are a G' (Lecky, 2019: 2) read the acknowledge-ments, where authorial and narratorial voice merge. Finally, the story unfolds in 'a context or environment with which [the playwright is] signally familiar' – council estates[19] in East London – and is thus told in what Katie Beswick (2014) calls the playwright's 'authentic voice'. For Beswick (98), the deployment of 'authentic voice' on stage has the effect of 'the playwright's own experience and history becom[ing] tied up with the perceived authenticity of the story'. *Superhoe*'s reception confirms this through the sheer volume of interviewers asking Lecky variations on the question: 'was that you at any time?' (Garvey, 2019: 27:50) and, following the launch of *Mood*, of articles promising Lecky's testimony on 'which aspects of her character are drawn from her own experience' (Hill-Paul, 2022).

On the other hand, the story Lecky tells – a morality tale of online sex work – is decidedly not her own. It belongs, rather, to anonymous 'camgirls', whom Lecky spoke to 'on snapchat and on Twitter', and whose stories she felt 'compelled to share' (Kelly, 2019) – as she clarifies also in a Q&A video featured on the Royal Court's website.[20] The play is thus the 'authentic story' of one, collective subject told by the 'authentic voice' of another, with auto-fictionality smoothing over the disjunction between the two, united by their marginalisation. In other words, Lecky's 'voice' – both embodied and disem-bodied – authenticates the character through the factuality of the playwright's lived experience, while telling a fictionalised version of other people's stories. The play thus chimes with Dix's definition of autofiction as autobiography 'written in the subjunctive mood', that is, 'less concerned with faithfully reporting what its protagonist did, or even how that person thought and felt, and [...] more concerned with the speculative question of how that subject might respond to new and often imagined environments' (Dix, 2018: 6) – in this case, what might have happened to Lecky had she been exposed to the forms of exploitation to which her character falls prey. The real 'camgirls', in turn, ground the fictionalisation in fact, lending the play a degree of 'authenticity by proxy' (Goodling & Mark, 2022).

Superhoe illustrates the difference between the autobiographical and the autofictional, and the strategic authentication at the heart of the latter. Indeed, to receive this play as autobiographical, as many have, is to reproduce the belittling trend discussed in the Introduction, whereby marginalised writers 'are bedevilled by the expectation – from readers and critics – that their work is based in the reality of their own lives', resulting in 'a treasure hunt for the "real" in their imagined worlds, and a diminution of its importance' (Clark, 2018).

---

[19] British social housing.

[20] https://royalcourttheatre.com/whats-on/superhoe/.

To receive the play instead as autofictional is to recognise the author/performer's agency in deploying aspects of their own lived experience to authenticate a fictional story, facilitating a critical discussion thereof. At a time in which speaking *for* is increasingly problematised, the twofold authentication of *Superhoe*, along a gradient of shared marginalisation, arguably protects it from accusations of appropriation of the voices, traumas, and experiences of others.[21]

A second means of authentication on stage involves objects, such as props, costumes, photographs, and videos. These can be either dramatic, by which I mean naturalisable in the world of the drama; or theatrical, that is, belonging to the non-naturalistic level of performance. In both cases, they have an ambiguous ontological status. On the one hand, they are part of the drama/performance, fictionalised by their presence on stage; on the other, they serve as portals between the drama/performance and the extra-theatrical world, pointing to the material realities – the facts – undergirding the staged fiction. They thus function, I suggest, as forms of *material* metalepsis: a concretised version of Gérard Genette's notion of 'narrative metalepsis' (1988: 88). The term indicates boundary crossings between narrative levels, such as when a character from a frame narrative enters an embedded narrative, or when the fictional and real world mix (e.g., when a character breaks the fourth wall).[22] By virtue of autofiction's explicit rooting of the story in the referential ground of an authorial 'I', in theatres of autofiction it is the boundaries between real and fictional (rather than between frame and embedded narratives) that metalepsis tends to play on. Causing one level or world to bleed into the other, sustained metalepsis gives rise to 'the unacceptable and insistent hypothesis that the extradiegetic is perhaps always diegetic' (Genette, 1988: 88), thus, that the extra-theatrical is perhaps always theatrical and, in the case of autofiction, vice versa.

A range of materially metaleptic devices with authenticating properties feature in Ostermeier's two adaptations of Eribon's *Returning to Reims* (2017 and 2021, based on *Retour à Reims*, published in French in 2009), and of Louis's *Who Killed My Father* (*Qui a tué mon père* (2020), based on the 2018 novel). In the former's source text – an autotheoretical essay – Eribon recounts his journey back to his hometown in the wake of his father's death, following years of estrangement. Inspired by Ernaux and sociologist Pierre Bourdieu, the journey gives rise to a reflection on the disenfranchisement of the French working class and their turn to the far right, and on the interplay of class and sexuality in spurring the author's social ascent. Both versions of the

---

[21] For more on this, see Goodling & Mark.

[22] See, e.g., Fleabag's audience-facing commentary in the British TV series (2016).

adaptation are set in a recording studio, in which a film-maker and an actor – Nina Hoss in the first production, Isabelle Redfern in the second, playing (versions of) themselves – collaborate on recording the voice-over for a film adaptation of Eribon's text. In the play's first half, the actor reads excerpts of the text against video footage of Eribon's journey home and of his current Parisian lifestyle, as well as relevant scenes from working-class history and political protests. The second half consists of a discussion of Eribon's text and its politics between the film-maker, the recording studio owner, and the actor, who brings further autofictional material to bear on the source text: class-related in the first version and intersectional in the second, in which additional lines by Redfern and Amewu Nove (in the role of the recording studio owner) build on Eribon's reflections from a racialised perspective. The adaptation of *Who Killed My Father*, on the other hand, is a dramatic monologue: starring Louis himself, it was co-produced by the Schaubühne and Paris's Théâtre de la Ville. Against a similar backdrop of video footage, Louis revisits his deprived childhood and difficult relationship with his father, framing his own experience, in the wake of Eribon, in a history of classed violence.[23]

Both works grapple with the authors' experiences of growing up gay in underprivileged areas, becoming estranged from their families, then reconnecting with them, and both make use of video footage produced for the production. Featuring the author-character in the real-world locations evoked in the text, this footage belongs to the theatrical fiction but is also a trace of real events in the author-character's life, which is shaped in turn by their autofictional performance. We watch Eribon visiting his mother, then the two of them looking through old photographs, knowing all the while that this intimate scene is both part of the narrated rapprochement *and* a performance, enacted in the presence of a Schaubühne cameraperson. In an obvious homage to Eribon and Louis, the same set-up on stage and on camera – with the playwright visiting his mother, looking through old photographs, and confronting his family's homophobia – is featured in Falk Richter's *The Silence* (2023), produced by the Schaubühne and included in the *Theatertreffen*.[24] These videos concretise the Möbius strip of autofictionality, granting it an intermedial dimension. In Eribon's case, they merge life and its performance by restaging a lived experience (i.e., his actual journey home), which in turn displays the traces of, or prefigures, its (future) performative restaging. Louis, on the other hand, is filmed skipping along a beach, in leaps and bounds that signify freedom. Is this a performance? Is it proof of the freedom he feels, following his 'escape' and social ascent and

---

[23] My analyses are based on the Schaubühne run of all co-productions.

[24] A two-week festival featuring performances of the ten productions judged to be the previous season's best premieres.

captured serendipitously on camera? Or is it an expression of the freeing effects of autofictional expression itself – a moment of release, as the cameraperson's presence grants the author-character a sense of how far he has come?

Following Dan Rebellato (2009), the relationship between what is present on stage and what it signifies dramatically can be understood as metaphorical. Metaphors comprise a tenor, or the thing that is being described; a vehicle, or the symbol/image used to evoke a quality of that thing; and a *tertium comparationis*, or the quality evoked. The same goes for drama: what we perceive on stage is the vehicle, what it stands for is the tenor, and the qualities characterising the vehicle and attributed metaphorically to the tenor are the *tertium comparationis*. The vehicle of a potted plant on stage, for example, might signify a forest (its tenor), suggesting, through its *tertium comparationis* (i.e., the fact of being potted), the domestication of nature. Like much staged autofiction, *Who Killed My Father* plays with this metaphorical relationship, showing the (real-world) tenor of its prop-vehicles, which would generally be left to the imagination, *alongside* the vehicles themselves. A hallucinatory, twinned presence thus comes to replace a more traditional presence and absence, shifting the performance's ontological status from fiction to hyperreality through a twofold authenticating process.

Louis's costume, and his T-shirt in particular, illustrate this well. Against a backdrop of black-and-white video footage of winding roads and rows of identical houses in working-class, dormitory towns, Louis changes into a red, Pokémon T-shirt, ties it in a '90s knot, dons a wig, and dances to Britney Spears. This is the first of several dance routines, whose repetition harks back to a painful childhood incident recounted at the first dance's conclusion. As a child, the author/narrator had choreographed a routine to Aqua's 'Barbie Girl' to show his parents and their friends at a dinner party, but his father had been unable to look at him, ashamed of his camp mannerisms. This sequence – the video footage, the wig, the dancing, and the Pokémon T-shirt – juxtaposes a range of narrative levels through material metalepsis, or through the presence of objects that belong to a range of narrative levels at once: the extra-theatrical world in which these objects really exist; the dramatic world based in memory and biographical past; and the theatrical world of the present of performance, bound up with desire, trauma, and repetition. The staged video – which inhabits the interstitial space between Louis's past and the present of the performance – reminds us that the working-class milieu the author grew up in, described in the play's text, has a material reality, and that the author's relationship to that material reality has been and is being impacted by his autofictional performance. Its incorporation into the set provides a curated trace of the real, opening a factual portal between affluent West Berlin and impoverished Northern

France, thus illustrating how far Louis has come, literally and metaphorically. The blond wig, on the other hand, materialises Louis's childhood fantasies: his desire to play the glamorous, feminine pop star, freely expressed after years of shame and repression. This materialisation of a narrated fantasy translates the idea, underpinning many forms of autofictional writing, 'that desires and dreams are an intrinsic element of a person's existence and perhaps disclose more, and different, things about a person than mere biographical data in chronological order' (Wagner-Egelhaaf, 2022: 27). A similar approach casts the autofictional as a space to recuperate these desires, particularly those that struggled to find real-world acceptance, and grant them (fictional) closure. Rooted in the (potential) reality of past desire, the wig remains, however, in the representational sphere of theatrical fiction.

The same seems to apply initially to Louis's Pokémon T-shirt: an adult-sized costume (i.e., a metaphorical vehicle) that gets a few laughs in its signifying – with reference to young Louis's clothing (i.e., its tenor) – a caricature of childhood naivety (i.e., the metaphor's *tertium comparationis*). Yet, after an interlude recounting his father's traumatic upbringing, Louis returns to 'Barbie Girl' and to the scene of his early homophobic shaming. Projected behind him this time – and again in the play's final scene, discussed in Section 3.2 – is a photograph of him as a child, wearing the same red, Pokémon T-shirt, or rather an XS version of it.[25] The metaphor's vehicle – the adult T-shirt worn on stage – is thus authenticated through the forensic display of a trace of its tenor, mirroring the practice, prominent in French literary autofiction, of interweaving photography and narrative (see Marcus, 2022). Through this duplicated presence – the authenticated costume on the one hand, and a staged trace of its referent on the other – Louis's T-shirt becomes an objective correlative of the autofictional mode, in which each (fictional) vehicle is haunted by the ghost of its (real-world) tenor. The transubstantiation of the prop's tenor, conjured from the realm of the symbolic into an iterative re-enactment of the real, grants the autofictional act the qualities of a ritual.

While material metalepsis can open portals between real-world past and dramatic present, this is not the only temporal relationship through which markers of authentication operate. In Selina Thompson's play *salt.* (2016) – a one-woman show, performed first by Thompson and then by actor Rochelle Rose, and based on the playwright's journey by cargo ship between Britain, Ghana, and Jamaica, retracing the Transatlantic Slave Triangle – it is the materially metaleptic evocation of a post-performance future that makes manifest the production's political affordances. Thompson interweaves recounted experiences of racial abuse, the story of her transatlantic crossing, and

---

[25] See Figure 3.

a historical account of the slave trade. Throughout the performance, 'The Woman' – as she is referred to in the script – repeatedly puts on safety goggles and smashes a huge chunk of 'naturally formed' rock salt with a sledgehammer, invoking imperialism and racism under various guises (Thompson, 2018: 13, 29–32. See Figure 1).

The salt is a fictional prop: a vehicle with a range of tenors ranging from Europe to capitalism. Yet the final speech makes its metaleptic import clear:

> (*To the audience.*) I'm going to leave this space now. And you will too.
> And when the last of you has left, you close the space, and we are finished.
> But before you go, you will meet me, sitting there with a basket of salt.
> I ask you to take a piece, wrap it and keep it safe.
> The salt is not safe for you to eat, but that is not what it is for. To take it is to make a commitment to live, a commitment to the radical space of not moving on, and all that it can open.
> Salt to heal, salt to remember, salt for your bath, for your nourishment, and above all for your wounds. (Thompson, 2018: 51–52)

The Woman invites the audience into the 'radical space of not moving on' through deliberate appropriation of a metaleptic object that will outlive the fiction and endure as a factual trace. Evoked in the final speech, the real-world stakes of this 'radical space' authenticate the performance retroactively: its source material and its symbolism; the lived experience at its heart and its

Figure 1 Thompson smashes a chunk of rock salt in *salt*.
(Rich Lakos/ArenaPAL).

implications of co-responsibility. The salt as a fictional prop offers the spectator a portal out of the drama. Unlike Louis's T-shirt, however, it does not connect to a referential past, of which the Middle Passage has erased all trace, but to an indefinite, post-performance future. 'To be a descendant of slaves visiting Ghana as a site of ancestry', The Woman says, 'is to try to go somewhere that doesn't exist to look for somebody that no one has heard of' (35). For the spectators, then, taking a chunk of salt constitutes a performative promise of solidarity through 'not moving on', materialised in the shared-out fragments of a symbolic concretion, sedimented over time.

The metatheatrical import of this closing gesture connects to the third locus of authentication addressed in this section: metatheatre, or the dramatic equivalent of metafiction, which is seen in literary scholarship as overlapping with, or 'an enhancer of', the autofictional (Schmitt, 2022: 90). On stage, it can be obtained through explicit references to the performance – for example, through audience address, as at the end of *salt.* – or by referring to the production's broader context, including the theatre's institutional identity, its geographical and social location, or relevant current affairs. It overlaps with the other two forms of authentication, through people and through objects, which can in turn overlap.[26]

Continuing where the last analysed excerpt left off, *salt.*'s final scene heightens its metatheatricality by referring to its own status as a play, thereby paradoxically reassuring the audience of the authenticity of its material:

> Because three years ago, Selina went all that way, it took all that for
>   her to decide to live.
> Each word of it is true. All of it happened. And this?
> This is her monument.
> This is her act of remembrance.
> This is her grief.
> Entrusted to me, so that the task of carrying it might be communal
> Because this is our burden
> Sit with it
> Sit with the pain
> It doesn't go away
> But we are sitting with you.
> There is work to be done
> And we must go on.
> Thank you –
>   *The End.* (52)

---

[26] For example, when video footage features authenticating people *within* an authenticating object.

If 'each word of it is true', so are the play's more surreal sequences, such as when the protagonist drowns and then returns to life. This refers to a deeper kind of truth, beyond distinctions between fact and fiction: as Zeldin suggests, it is autofiction's sincerity rather than its referential accuracy that gets 'closer to the actual truth' (Crompton, 2023). Made into a 'monument', The Woman's grief is thus authenticated metatheatrically as Thompson's grief ('Selina/I went all the way'),[27] and the shared burden that the audience are invited to 'sit with', concretised in the lump of salt they take home, extracted sharply from the realm of the fictional.

Metafiction and metatheatre merge in Richter's *The Silence*, a one-man show marketed as autofictional that gives expression to what was left unsaid during the playwright's upbringing. Actor Dimitrij Schaad introduces the play, commenting on its sophistication as a cultural product in a blandishment to spectators that have chosen to attend. Having announced his transformation into the playwright, who appears later in video footage – 'I will now become Falk Richter' – Schaad tells the audience that the play will be about his (that is, Richter's) family, in which everyone always 'panicked they would end up in one of my plays'.[28] Metatheatrical irony is thus deployed from the outset to establish complicity with the spectator, who is first flattered, then frankly informed of the referential status of what is unfolding on stage. This frankness elicits willingness to indulge a radically subjective and aggrieved revisiting of what was and what could have been, which gains authenticity precisely by virtue of its detachment from the 'official' version of events, which – we are told – has long been enveloped in euphemism and the titular silence. By consistently communicating its referential ground – for example, when Schaad announces he is resuming Richter's story, following digressions about his own casting and background – the play situates itself metatheatrically as a form of working through in which the spectator is explicitly asked to bear witness to a different kind of truth: the playwright's right to feel and think radically on his own terms.

Finally, in *Das Ereignis* (2023), the Berliner Ensemble's adaptation of Ernaux's *L'événement* (2000)/*Happening* (2001), the story is authenticated through the classically metatheatrical device of juxtaposing the time and place of the drama (1960s France) with the time and place of the performance (2020s Germany). About halfway through the dramatisation – a monologue, shared between three women, of Ernaux's account of her own illegal abortion – one actor interrupts Ernaux's story by reciting the anti-abortion laws in force in France in the 1960s, thus evoking the socio-political context that caused Ernaux

---

[27] Depending on whether Thompson or Rose is performing.

[28] All translations of quotations from Schaubühne productions are my own.

to seek the traumatic and life-threatening intervention whose subjective dimension is at the heart of the text and play. While this first interruption remains *within* the dramatic setting – it ends with the words 'France, 1963' – it is followed in chiastic symmetry by another legal text, beginning with the words 'Germany, 2023'. The reactionary language and content of contemporary abortion law in the production's national context serves to authenticate it, moving the story sharply from the past tense of fiction, known to elicit an 'attitude of detachment' in the receiver (Ricœur, 1990: 189), into the present of political debate.

Whether signalled through people, objects, or metatheatrical play, authenticity on stage is strategic. Yet its staged forms often draw on (painful or traumatic) lived experience, and – crucially – are not always freely chosen by those whose life is drawn on. As discussed in the Introduction and returned to in Section 4, authenticity's cultural market value, predicated on its promise of intimate self-revelation – which can 'feel' political without threatening societal structures, and testify to cultural inclusion – heightens demand, particularly in connection with marginalisation, trauma, and victimhood. Increasingly deployed in the creative industries as a de facto synonym of diversity, authenticity has thus become, for many marginalised creatives, a condition to fulfil in order to be able to speak (see Goodling & Mark, 2022). Markers of fictionalisation thus play a vital role in autofiction's critical affordances, extracting it from the realm of the confessional, as the next section explores.

2.2 Markers of Fictionalisation

Discussions of fiction in theatre require some conceptual clarification. Like James, I use 'fictionalisation' to emphasise 'the transposition of real-life elements into fictional form' (Effe & Lawlor, 2022: 7), with 'fictionality', in contrast, indicating their wholesale invention. While the boundaries between the two are blurred, a distinction between what is at work in *Harry Potter* (a fictional universe of magical creatures) as opposed to Knausgaard's *My Struggle* (an obviously stylised attempt to recapture the author's life in minute detail) proves intuitive and analytically useful. The performing arts, then, require a further distinction: between dramatic and theatrical fiction. With reference to Theresia Birkenhauer, Zipfel (2014: 111–112) explains how 'dramatic fiction points to the fictionality of the semantic content of the written play and highlights that the presented story or storyworld is fictional', while 'theatrical fiction' indicates 'the fact that the representation of a story on the stage produces a specific performance world'. Inasmuch as the latter applies to every piece of theatre, the former plays a more significant role in suggesting the presence of the autofictional on stage. Particularly in the presence of the autofictional, however, the two are often not so neatly separable, and theatrical fiction, too, can be accentuated or toned down in ways that influence the spectator's attitude to the dramatic material. 'Temporal experimentation', for example, and 'departure from a linear, sequential, chronological time frame' (Dix, 2018: 2) characterise autofiction on stage as much as on the page and can heighten spectatorial perception of the work of fictionalisation.

Murray's account of making *DenMarked* offers a wealth of insights into the negotiation of authenticity and fictionalisation from a position of marginalisation in the creative industries. Recounting the development of the production, which began as a short monologue for the 2013 London Stories Festival and was then commissioned by the Battersea Arts Centre and developed through the institution's trademark 'scratch' process,[29] Murray admits he 'made the show after being coerced into doing it': though he initially 'didn't want to', he gave in for 'the money' (Beswick & Murray, 2022: 158–160). Indeed, having put his brother forward, Murray was encouraged to contribute himself by drawing on his own experience:

> And then the producer of the festival said, 'But you've got so many stories, just tell one of your stories.' And I was like, 'Huh?' And he went, 'You're always telling stories, just do one of them.' And I just off the cuff said, 'Well my dad went to jail at Christmas.' And then another producer went, 'Just tell that story then, what's the story?' And I said, 'I have always dreamed about going to prison. But I guess a lot of people have that dream. I guess it's to do with my dad going to jail at Christmas – I mean, everyone's got that similar story about when their dad left or whatever, it's just gonna be cliché.' And they were, like, 'No, no. Tell that story, tell that story.' And I was, like, 'Oh. Okay.' The money was quite good. £500 or something to write this five-minute story.' (Beswick & Murray, 2022: 158)

Beginning at commission, the catch-22 of the authenticity economy comes full circle in *DenMarked*'s production and reception. Encouraged and ·offered money by industry gatekeepers to draw on his experience, Murray is at once lauded when the rawness of his material shines through – he recounts having 'had a break down' in an early performance, overwhelmed by his own 'intense stories', then being told by spectators who saw the show again that 'they preferred it that time' (162–163) – and criticised for being unable to move beyond the confessional, as in the Tom Thumb Theatre Q&A. Conversely, many writers of autofiction are accused of fictionalisation when their material does not 'feel' authentic enough. Louis, for example, describes editors' reactions to his

---

[29] That is, incorporating feedback on the work-in-progress through ad hoc performances to industry people and staff, thus permitting significant institutional control.

first novel, *En finir avec Eddy Bellegueule* (2014) or *The End of Eddy* (2017), about his early experiences of poverty and homophobia: 'Editors would refuse the manuscript, saying, Poor people aren't like that! They'd grown up in a wealthy environment. They'd never known or even seen poverty, but they wanted me to respect their image and myths about the poor – filth, working-class solidarity, enjoyment of life, and so on' (Louis & Taïa, 2018). Working-class writer, performer, and screenwriter Cash Carraway has also been the target of online speculation on her work's authenticity, as well as full-blown witch hunts. Beswick recounts how:

> Carraway was the victim of an online stalker, a middle class 'mummy blogger', famous in the online sphere – who has publicly spammed message boards such as mums net and tattle life with the claims that Carraway is not working class at all, her whole life is a lie, and demanded that her publishing contracts are rescinded. This campaign led to a national newspaper investigating Carraway for literary forgery. In response Carraway has defended the veracity of her memoir writing – but the word 'memoir' has been removed from the subtitle of the paperback (changed to *Notes from the Poverty Line*). Her play, *Refuge Woman*, has been retitled as: *Refuge Woman: A- Fucking-Fictional- Play & Other Poverty Porn Stories*.[30]

In such contexts of power imbalances between a marginalised author and industry gatekeepers/audiences, fictionalisation has particularly high stakes. It allows the author (to attempt, at least) to extract their work from the realm of the confessional, foregrounding its artfulness and displaying awareness of the curated nature of any self-storytelling act, as well as of the creative industries' exploitative dynamics, gestured to in Carraway's ironic change of title. Moreover, it can offer a means for writers to acknowledge – and at times even try to address – the ethical and political problems undergirding their work.

Like authenticity, however, not every form of fictionalisation is freely chosen or empowering, particularly when unmarked. Murray recounts the reshaping of his dramatic material by the creative team, who – he explains – 'understands a middle-class audience a lot more than I do' (Beswick & Murray, 2022: 162). His account of stealing, for example, was cut by the director, who said it would make it 'hard to like [him]', while his abusive father and stepfather were compressed into one character, with Murray's editor explaining that '[h]aving one abusive dad makes more sense than having two!' (161–162). These edits serve the explicit purpose of catering to an imagined, middle-class audience, putting them at ease, eliciting their sympathies, and excising anything disruptive of pitch-perfect victimhood.

---

[30] See Beswick's unpublished paper, available at: https://ualresearchonline.arts.ac.uk/id/eprint/17645/3/Cash%20Carraway%20sex%20lies%20and%20difficult%20truths.pdf.

These behind-the-scenes edits contrast with *DenMarked*'s overt markers of fictionalisation. Indeed, shaping the play is an intertextual dialogue, in which episodes of Murray's life, narrated on stage, are shored up and re-signified through excerpts and references to *Hamlet*. Through Shakespeare, Murray reflects on (narrative) constructions of selfhood and their role in determining what one feels entitled or destined to, or the ways in which one is *den-marked*. Murray's account of the production process is, again, revealing:

> I was scared, because I'm terrible at Shakespeare. Who wants to sit there and see me do Shakespeare? Look at me. People who love Shakespeare do not want to watch me do Shakespeare. Not really. So, I was like, 'Fuck. Shit. I don't even think [Battersea Arts Centre] are going to like this idea.' And they didn't. The first thing was: 'No. We like you rapping. We like you telling dirty stories, but Shakespeare? People that like Shakespeare, theatre people, they're not gonna like this. You're not good. You can't even talk right anyway. Let alone do Shakespeare. (Beswick & Murray, 2022: 160)

Like in the Carraway witch hunt, what emerges here are the clear-cut boundaries of the right to fiction: to dabble with (highbrow) culture, to inscribe one's life within canonical narratives, to rarefy one's experience in fictional terms are not devices to which everyone is welcome. The right to fictionalisation is, in short, inversely proportional to the requirement to be authentic. One's entitlement to the former and freedom from the latter depend on one's place on a spectrum from privilege to marginalisation, linked to race, class, gender, sexuality, and (dis)ability. And indeed, the edits suggested to Murray serve to reinforce rather than disrupt the text's authenticity. Yet it is Shakespeare rather than the recurring nightmare of ending up in jail that secures Murray's investment in the project: 'once I started mixing the Shakespeare, I had a concept and I was like, I really like this. Even if other people hate it, I don't care now, because I think this is clever' (160).

The stakes of fictionalisation from a racialised perspective are palpable in both *salt.* and Arinzé Kene's *Misty* (2018). Towards the end of *salt.*, the story veers off into a dream-like sequence. The Woman jumps off the ship into the mass grave of the sea and '*drowns*' – as the stage directions read, '*and her body becomes salt*', then is brought back to life by the voice of her 'nan' and the hands of her forebears, who remind her 'how sacred it is to be a descendent of those that were never supposed to survive' (50–51). Here and elsewhere, *salt.* reflects the definition of autofiction as works in which 'the *what* of the narrative refers to real persons and events, at times painstakingly so' while 'the *how* of the narrative resembles experimental fiction: anti-retrospection, unmarked transitions between visions, dreams, and events, etc.' (Iversen, 2020: 556). Through its markers of surreal fictionalisation, the drowning scene deviates from a realist narrative, foregrounding the latter's limits, the illusion of form and logic fostered thereby. The play thus refuses the neat temporal and causal nexuses – that simplify, obfuscate, and drive towards resolution – through which a subject is expected to situate itself in history. The radical time and space of 'not moving on' is opened on stage by sidestepping the (white) conventions of teleological narrative, all the more alien to those whose past has been violently erased and whose future unfolds in the knowledge they were 'never supposed to survive'. Outside the logic of realist narrative, the Woman is thus at once dead and alive; flesh and salt; Selina and not Selina; her play not merely 'a true story' but – like the cleansing act she performs at the show's opening – a form of ritual, beginning without ending in an individual.

First staged at London's Bush Theatre, *Misty* also sidesteps the racialised traps of realist narrative through markers of fictionalisation embedded in ostensibly authentic material. In it, black playwright and performer Arinzé Kene tells the story of black playwright Arinzé, who is struggling to write a play that is political and true to his experience, but also steers clear of 'modern minstrel show' tropes (Kene, 2018: 18), that sell out (his community) and solidify racial stereotypes among white audiences. In the script's Preface, Kene recounts how the play was inspired by conversations with fellow theatre-makers Donna and Raymond about the absurdity of the category of 'black plays'. He clarifies that Raymond's 'name ain't actually Raymond, I've changed it to protect his identity' (7), then that the same goes for Donna, thereby implying the referential reality of the people represented, thus the factual nature of the Preface as a whole. Soon, however, the story takes on parodic tones: overwhelmed by her questioning of the politics of racialising labels, Donna ends up becoming 'neither an actress, or a black actress' but 'a shit actress': 'Never in the moment, never in the scene. Only ever thinking about her blackness' (10). These signs of fictionalisation are confirmed by a strong metaleptic reversal at the Preface's conclusion: 'Maybe Donna's made up. I don't know. She's real somewhere. Anyway. Whatever happened, it led me to write this thing' (10). Kene thus justifies his play through an allegedly true story, only to then expose this story as made up, raising the question of why his text, more than any other, should require rooting in the real.

The same dynamic is reproduced in the play itself through continuous referential and metaleptic slippages: between authentication and fictionalisation, and between the various narrative levels of the drama. Donna and Raymond reappear as characters: they are now a couple and represent Arinzé's community, suspicious of the politics of his 'black' writing. Increasingly surreal, the scenes dramatising the difficulty of Arinzé's creative process – caught between the rock of his friends, who accuse him of selling out, and the hard place of white industry gatekeepers, hungry for his 'authentic' material – are juxtaposed with scenes from his work-in-progress, which tells the story of Virus: a black, socially disadvantaged youth who gets into trouble. Again, Virus is initially authenticated: in response to his friends' accusation that Virus is a stereotype – the white fantasy of an angry black man – Arinzé explains that he is based on a real person, Lucas, killed by gang violence, so cannot be reduced to a racist trope. In symmetry with the Preface, however, this is soon contradicted: like Donna and Raymond, Lucas turns out to be a fake referent, made up to authenticate the story Arinzé simply wants to tell, beyond the burden of representation he carries.

The play's dramatis personae are all ontologically unstable: whether figments of the playwright's imagination like Lucas; surreally staged like Arinzé's adult sister, played by a ten-year-old in reading glasses (32–34); or reduced to grotesque caricatures, like the industry gatekeepers who spout a nonsensical pastiche of Hollywood clichés (56–58), their slippery, metatheatrical status rubs off onto Kene's autofictional 'I', which cannot be taken too literally. The performance is thus established as a ludic space in which the dramatic material is constantly exposed as phoney. This facilitates a kaleidoscopic exploration of the paradox of self-expression in an industry that sells storified selves, an exploration that is safeguarded by its refusal to let any material or identity that has been authenticated linger for too long, like the real-world referents of Donna and Raymond, which are rapidly unsettled. Fittingly, the play's conclusion consists of a freeing, irreverent rap, in which Arinzé invites those who 'don't like [his] theatre shit' to 'suck [his] big black theatre dick' (71), letting go with jubilant playfulness of his attempts to 'get it right' as a black playwright. Kene thus finds freedom in fiction, releasing the pressure of his writing commission like air from the balloons he bursts gleefully on stage. The playful yet poignant reclamation of his unencumbered right to stories is facilitated by a sustained commitment to what Jean-Marie Schaeffer (2010) calls 'shared ludic feint': an investment in fiction, in other words, as a legitimate means to truth, or a reappropriation of the (racialised) self as a locus not of testimony but of play.

As this section has shown, the oscillation between testimony and play undergirds autofiction and its political affordances at large. A focus on the interactions between authenticating devices, which disrupt the 'attitude of detachment' (Ricœur, 1990: 189) elicited by fiction, and markers of fictionalisation (which destabilise the urge to fuse author and character) facilitates nuanced and materially grounded analysis by attending to authorial agency in the deployment of lived experience within an artistic and political project. The section's case studies considered the interplay of authenticity and fictionalisation in rooting the autofictional self in its referential ground. Authenticating through the self *only* is what allows Kene's play, for example, to reach its liberating conclusion, having freed all other characters from any referential ground by exposing them as mere narrative devices. Where clearly identified real-world referents *are* evoked on stage, however, oscillations between fact and fiction have different implications. The next section will dig into this difference, exploring the negotiation of selfhood and otherness in theatres of autofiction, and the role of fact/fiction therein.

3 Self/Other

Unusually explicit in his ambition to find a way of 'doing' autofiction in the theatre, Alexander Zeldin was inspired in making *The Confessions* (2023), a play based on his mother's life, by Rachel Cusk's notion of the self as an outline, introduced in the eponymous first volume of her trilogy (2014). Narrated by a woman called Faye, the three novels consist almost entirely of conversations with people Faye encounters. Often in response to Faye's questions, these 'others' deliver long and detailed accounts of (meaningful episodes of) their lives. Faye, on the other hand, reveals little, acting more as a 'coaxer' (Przulj, 2022), projecting surface, and reteller of others' stories, which are recounted in the novels through a mixture of direct, free indirect, and reported speech, making the voice of Faye and her interlocutors hard to distinguish. The reader discerns something of Faye's identity through her acts of narrative reception, making her out not as a fully fledged character but as an outline, in contrast with and in response to the detailed stories of others. Faye is thus perceptible only relationally, through the effects others' stories have on her, and through the traces of her revealed in the novels' ventriloquistic (re)telling. Like Cusk, Zeldin set out to stage a 'shape that was not filling in all the dots but was drenched in experience and the body and the feeling of being in a space' (Crompton, 2023): the shape of an ordinary woman, remarkable not in its detail but in its ability to evoke a generation, a *zeitgeist*. Alongside his mother's story, drawn out in preparatory interviews, the plot contains 'a lot that is made up'. The ensuing play is 'a kind of dance with truth', which hopes to lead, Zeldin suggests, 'closer to the actual truth'.

While Zeldin's process echoes the narrative practices of literary autofiction, not all of them translate on stage. In *The Confessions*, the autofictional is evoked mainly by the frame narrative, in which (an actor playing) Zeldin's elderly mother responds to silent questions. 'I'm an old lady. What's interesting about me? I have nothing of interest to tell you', she tells the audience at the play's opening, as though they had invited her to speak. Except for the play's final moments, featuring the character of young Zeldin, the playwright's role as the (absent) 'coaxer' of the titular confessions remains invisible, hanging spectrally over the audience. Embedded in this frame, the play unfolds, however, largely realistically, recounting scenes from a life whose autofictional import is lost on anyone unaware of the playwright's ambitions. This is because Zeldin's attempt to adapt Cusk's device inverts the self/other relationship at its heart. In Cusk's trilogy, it is Faye, the author's avatar, who becomes visible as an outline – a 'shape [...] drenched in experience' – in contrast with the detailed self-narration of others. While Zeldin adopts Cusk's model, he does so in the frame narrative only, and with the intention of 'outlining' not his autofictional self but its interlocutor. Missing from the equation, then, is the listening/receiving self, without which an outline 'drenched in experienced' and evoked through its perception of others seems elusive if not impossible to stage.

The relationship between self and other in theatres of autofiction is twofold. It involves the autofictional self first opening itself up to a collective on the basis of sameness – becoming, in other words, transpersonal – then encountering alterity in the form of an 'other'. This section focuses on each process in turn, reflecting on their aesthetics and politics across this Element's corpus, before providing a more in-depth case study for each. Akin to fact/fiction, the boundaries between self and other can be blurred to varying degrees: at one end of the spectrum are plays where the entire dramatic world feels coextensive with the mind of the protagonist, as in *The Writer*, discussed in the first section. At the other are plays in which clearly identified real-world others are fictionalised, as in Louis's *History of Violence* – published in French in 2016 and adapted in 2018 at the Schaubühne – discussed at length in Section 3.2.

3.1 The Transpersonal Self

For James (2022: 48), the 'fundamental contradiction of autofiction', identified by Genette in the mode's assertion that '"[i]t is I and it is not I," [...] does not open a breach at the level of the text's pragmatic contract, but rather functions on the thematic level to express a non-unitary conception of the self'. In other words, it is less a matter of misleading the reader than of projecting a narratorial self that is at once radically subjective and open enough to stand in for a collective based on shared experience: less a specific individual than a type. Writing against the label of autofiction, Ernaux speaks eloquently of this process in her own practice: the 'I' of her fiction, she writes (2019), is 'an impersonal form, barely gendered [...]: a transpersonal form, in short. It's not a way of building an identity for myself, through a text, of autofictionalizing myself, but a way of grasping, within my experience, the signs of a family, social or passionate reality.' In other words, the self holds a narrative trace of a set of experiences, whose transpersonal resonance is at the heart of the autofictional, particularly in its more recent, sociologically invested and politicised forms, often issuing from a place of marginalisation.

Constructed in this way, the autofictional self feels relatable as it is at once authentic – that is, 'drenched in experience', to return to Zeldin's phrase – *and* generic enough to be transpersonal, like Cusk's outlines. It has, in other words, the affective resonance of intimate self-expression coupled with the legibility of a 'type'. This is not too far from the relational dynamics of social media stories discussed in the Introduction, wherein relatability is predicated on a mixture of performed 'authenticity' and (self-)standardising scripts. The autofictional self thus becomes 'an ambiguous space of projection, positioned between the individual and the collective' (James, 2022: 49) – or at least *a* collective – credible inasmuch as it is 'drenched' in the former, and relatable and politicised, particularly in recent autofiction, inasmuch as it positions itself within, gains resonance from, and opens up to the latter.

The same is true on stage, where the embodied dimension of the medium adds several representational layers. When spoken by a specific body, the transpersonal 'I' loses the indeterminacy it has in print. If Cusk's Faye were standing in front of us, we would be confronted with far more defined attributes (her voice, appearance, etc.) than the elusive nature of her textual presence reveals. In the theatre, then, the self must gesture beyond the body that represents it to become what Ernaux calls the sign 'of a family, social or passionate reality', making explicit which set of experiences it stands for through a range of dramatic or textual devices. The Berliner Ensemble's adaptation of Ernaux's *Happening*, for example, dramatises the self's transpersonal dimension by having not one but three actors speaking Ernaux's autofictional 'I', embodying the 'enunciative gap' present therein (James, 2022: 49). The juxtaposition of French and German abortion law builds further on this, poignantly connecting the singular/plural woman-subject speaking (in) the text and embodied on stage with the women-object spoken *about* and *for* by the respective legal texts.

In recent theatres of autofiction, the experiences the self stands in for tend to be less existential or emotive (e.g., Ernaux's 'passions'), and more shaped by identity politics: linked to marginalisation, as the rest of this section illustrates, or to marginalisation *and* national and generational trauma, as exemplified by *The Silence*. Indeed, all the plays in this Element's corpus signal their political commitment through the explicit inscription of the self within a transpersonal collective identified on the basis of class, gender, sexuality, and/or race. This is done in a range of ways. In *DenMarked*, for instance, the autofictional self inscribes itself into the classed collective of those predestined to reproduce a script that has become, as Murray points out, a cliché: a repetition of trauma and violence that culminates in 'going to prison' (Beswick & Murray, 2022: 158). The transpersonal resonance of the play's subject is suggested in its title, which promises the story of those who move through life with a constrained horizon, *marked* as they are by their '*den*'. In dialogue with *Hamlet* – arguably, the most celebrated exploration of interiority in the Western dramatic canon, with whose much-touted 'universality' only some, as Murray makes clear, are allowed to identify – the play's intertextual structure validates the right to an alternative for the transpersonal subject(s) at its heart, despite their *den-marked* beginnings.

The self in *Superhoe*, too, becomes transpersonal through shared marginal-isation along classed, racialised, and gendered lines and, like *DenMarked*, its affective power also rests on two possible 'outcomes' for those included in the transpersonal collective. The 'enunciative gap' in Lecky's 'I' derives from, among other things, the blending of Lecky and the anonymous 'cam girls' on whose stories the playwright drew. As discussed in Section 2, their shared marginalisation facilitates the play's 'authenticity by proxy', encompassing two storylines that begin parallel and then branch off in opposite directions. Indeed, from a shared position of social marginalisation, the story of the 'cam girls' descends into a spiral of abuse, while Lecky moves upwards via the theatre into television success, offering an affectively rewarding counter-narrative to the story unfolding on stage – a dynamic the next section will nuance.

Something slightly different is at work in Falk Richter's *The Silence*. While the autofictional self does situate itself in a queer community through experiences of homophobic violence, equally if not more important to its transpersonal capaciousness are legacies of inherited trauma on a generational scale. In other words, alongside identity-related marginalisation, it is the experience of living in the wake and shadow of WWII and the Holocaust that the autofictional self becomes a vehicle for. This is conveyed in the production via a series of fictional conversations between Richter and his deceased father, enacted by the actor playing the 'autofictional playwright', as Richter is repeatedly referred to. These conversations return to moments in Richter's past – his father's death among them – and veer off into fiction, rewriting events. Richter's father is thus made to express the things he was never able to voice (as Richter imagines them): from his war-related trauma to his consequent inability to love his son. Schaad-as-Richter then reflects mournfully that 'I would have understood', 'but unfortunately it wasn't like that': in fact, 'he didn't say any of this. I have to put these words in his mouth today'. Autofiction thus facilitates a posthumous un-silencing of the war generation, recasting the staged, quintessentially

German self as a locus of transpersonal reckoning with the legacies of inherited trauma and guilt on a generational, and thus national, scale. As the staged self is chorally refracted – like in Ernaux's *Happening* – through the simultaneous presence on stage of an actor playing Richter and footage of the real Richter, and takes shape less through the detail of individual experiences and personality than through the traces of others imprinted on it, it forms less a specific character than a transpersonal outline, 'drenched', as per Zeldin's ambition, 'in experience and the body'.

Richter's autofictional self dominates *The Silence* almost entirely. There is, however, one significant exception: the footage of the playwright's mother, in which a real-world 'other' breaks the solipsism of the performance space. With her voice, body, and different take on the story told, she underscores the radically subjective, generational space of the play by foregrounding its limits. She represents, in short, another version of events, another set of incommensurable lived experiences: the transpersonal collective of those who belong to a previous generation and cannot identify with the staged self. Kene's *Misty* and Hickson's *The Writer*, on the other hand, let the solipsistic space of the self dominate the performance entirely, with no real-world other to disrupt it. The autofictional self is thus all-encompassing and gives rise to a modern-day, autofictional Psychomachia of sorts,[31] in which all dramatis personae – even those antagonising the protagonist – come across as voices in a mindscape. In these and similar cases, the self becomes transpersonal through processes of narrative rarefaction, which reduce it to a dramatic avatar: the representative on stage of a (marginalised) type, as illustrated by the following analysis of *The Writer*. With an in-depth discussion of this section's final case study, I aim to explore the dramatic workings of the transpersonal self in more granular detail, illustrating how theatres of autofiction gesture beyond the individual, rarefy it into a type, and foreground the 'enunciative gap' in the 'I' spoken on stage.

Produced at a range of international venues following its London premiere, Hickson's *The Writer* is – in its Almeida run, at least[32] – an autofictional play about a playwright writing an autofictional play. By embedding autofiction within autofiction, *The Writer* doubly refracts the lived experience at the heart of the material, conjuring less an individual than an ontologically unstable type

---

[31] A 'conflict of the soul' like the medieval morality play *Everyman*, in which inner struggles are externalised and personified.

[32] As autofictionality is context dependent, it varies from production to production. In *The Writer*, it is predicated on the playwright's and artistic director's notoriety in the British theatre scene, on the play's metatheatrical references, and on the industry conditions represented on stage, thus heightened in its original production, on which my analysis is based. The Berliner Ensemble production (2022), on the other hand, was marketed and received in the German context largely as a work of dramatic fiction.

Figure 2 A young woman and older man face off in Ella Hickson's *The Writer* at the Almeida Theatre (Manuel Harlan/ArenaPAL).

or test subject for a thought experiment that subsumes all other characters into its orbit. Akin to *Misty*, *The Writer*, too, fits Dix's definition of autofiction as autobiography 'written in the subjunctive mood', that is, 'less concerned with faithfully reporting what its protagonist did, or even how that person thought and felt, and [...] more concerned with the speculative question of how that subject might respond to new and often imagined environments' (Dix, 2018: 6) – the performance comprising an internally focalised[33] sequence of the latter.

The play begins in an empty theatre. A performance has just finished; a young woman re-enters the auditorium where she has forgotten her bag and catches sight of an older man (see Figure 2). 'Hi', he says; 'Hi', she replies (11). The man wants to know what she made of the evening's show; she caricatures it as follows:

> Two people walking on stage and pretending to be two other people and saying – 'Hi', 'hi' – or worse – much fucking worse, walking on stage and – (*Beat*.) 'Phil looks uncomfortable in his skin, beat, Phil fiddles with his lighter but doesn't light the cigarette, beat' because we all know cigarettes need a licence to be lit and Cara enters – 'thunderously sexual, beat', whatever that fucking means, what does that even mean? (Hickson, 2018: 13)

---

[33] For example, when the Writer's partner confronts her with normative milestones she does not desire (marriage, reproduction, etc.), a crying baby – which her partner does not see or hear – becomes audible and is then passed to the Writer. This is a dramatic equivalent of internal focalisation.

The scene works both metatheatrically and autofictionally. On the one hand, in ridiculing what Cusk might call the fake and embarrassing conventions of British realism, the young woman becomes a mouthpiece for Hickson's frustration. 'It's you that gets to make the world and me that's got to live in it', the young woman tells the older man (15); the same, as is implied, goes for playwriting. Cited at the beginning of this Element, her ruthless indictment of contemporary theatre goes on to contrast Trump and other contemporary 'monstrosities' (14) with the industry's bloodless attempts to entertain. Hickson's own voice is audible in the young woman's, in an early sign of autofictionality. 'I've got to the point where I hate theatre, like everything I go and see is awful', the playwright admits in a pre-show discussion, available on the Almeida's website (31:08), making similar claims on other fora.[34] On the other hand, from their very first 'hi's, the two characters engage in dialogue that works precisely *because* it rests on the dramatic apparatus that is being ridiculed. Hickson's autofictional avatar thus reveals at once the playwright's frustration with, *and* reproduction of, the 'intellectual back-and-forth', whose 'dialectic' and 'wordy' 'power struggle', despite its elitism and patriarchal undertones, fits the British 'definition of good drama' (67). Here and throughout the play, two contradictory positions are played off against each other ironically in an autofictional conflict with metatheatrical stakes: the urge to destroy and reinvent frameworks of value, and the urge to be successful and recognised within the old ones.

Intrigued and (alas unsurprisingly) aroused by the woman's frustration and impassioned earnestness – she wants 'the world to change shape'; to 'dismantle capitalism and overturn the patriarchy' (19, 23) – the man, who turns out to be the theatre's artistic director, offers her an open commission. This heightens the scene's autofictionality, as *The Writer* is itself the result of an open commission offered by the Almeida's (older, male) artistic director, Rupert Goold, to a (younger, female) playwright. Like Hickson's, the woman's gendered anger is 'zeitgeisty' and a highly valued currency in today's creative industries; it will, in the director's words, get 'bums on seats' (21). The two go on to hotly debate the industry's gender politics until their sparring is interrupted by two more actors joining them on stage: the Writer and the Director of the scene we have just witnessed, which is revealed as the Writer's work-in-progress: a play within the play. This new frame narrative sees the four characters – the Writer and Director of the previous scene, alongside the actors who played the young woman and older man – sit down for a post-show, 'scratch'-like discussion, to

---

[34] Including social media and interviews (e.g., Angel-Perez, Rousseau & Ayache, 2023). For the pre-show Q&A, see www.youtube.com/watch?v=jJZi5xCfspQ&t=18s&ab_channel=AlmeidaTheatre.

elicit feedback from the audience. The discussion features a toned-down version of the power dynamics palpable and railed against in the previous scene, commenting – again metatheatrically – on the proximity between what is represented and its material conditions of production.

Juxtaposing scenes from the titular Writer's work-in-progress (Acts One and Three), with scenes in which the Writer discusses her work with the commissioning Director (Acts One and Four) and with two different romantic partners: a man (Act Two), then a woman (Act Five), *The Writer* tells the story of a woman's struggles to write a play that feels authentic and reflects her politics under patriarchal capitalism. More than anything else, however, *The Writer* dramatises an autofictional writing process. We watch a writer engage in a self-fictionalising practice, and recognise ideas, feelings, and images as they recur between scenes: expressed first by the Writer's fictional character (the young woman), then by the Writer herself, on the Möbius strip of intradiegetic autofiction.

As Act One exemplifies, *The Writer* not only dramatises autofictional play-writing, but works autofictionally too. Its autofictionality is thus twofold: the Writer is an autofictional version of Hickson, while her character, the young woman, is an autofictional version of an autofictional version of Hickson, a Platonic 'copy of a copy' of the real-world playwright. Indeed, Hickson's own opinions, turns of phrase, and frustrations resonate on stage in the words of both the (fictional) Writer and her character, just like the critical voice of the Director comes across – in the autofictional space – more as self-criticism placed in the mouth of an imagined, male 'other' than as something the autofictional 'I' can entirely reject.[35] The stage – with its increasingly surreal set, suggestive less of a coherent storyworld than of a nightmarish mindscape – thus becomes coextensive with the internal struggles of a generic self, and the various characters mere aspects thereof, personifications in a Psychomachia. As the metatheatrical reversals reflect and refract it, the autofictional self is reduced to a gendered, raced outline: not a fully fledged individual but the contours of something more capacious. She is a white, middle-class feminist; she is creative, angry, cramped by societal strictures, and aware of the limits of her politicised writing, the compromises of her industry involvement, and the egotism of her own desire for relevance. She is and is not Hickson, inviting (some) spectators in. Indeed, as Section 4 will explore, there are clear limits as to who can recognise themselves in the transpersonal self.

I have shown how Hickson's doubly self-fictionalising play absorbs all alterity into the orbit of the outlined self. Even the antagonistic Director, casting

---

[35] As confirmed by Hickson (see Angel-Perez, Rousseau & Ayache, 2023: 229).

doubt on the Writer's intentions, is merely one of many voices that can be traced back to the playwright, who remains, like in *Misty*, the principal referent of the fiction. A different dynamic undergirds most theatres of autofiction, which tend to grapple meta-reflexively with the representation of real-world others. This is the second way in which the autofictional self opens itself relationally: having defined those it is *similar to*, it outlines itself against those it is *different from*, as detailed in the next section.

3.2 Staging Others, Telling Otherwise

'How do we become something other than what we are', asks Louis in conversation with writer Abdellah Taïa in *The Paris Review* (2018); 'how do we become something other than what the world has made of us?'. Both writers find an answer in the autofictional: with its oscillatory movements between fact and fiction, it is less a form of confession than of what Paul Ricœur calls '*telling otherwise*' (1999: 9, emphasis original): a politicised harnessing of fictionalisation. Their hope is that this might lead, on the Möbius strip of autofictional writing, to *being* otherwise, or being other.

While issuing from an individual, the autofictional 'I' can and indeed should, for Louis and Taïa, become a mouthpiece for a pain that is and is not their own. Populating the autofictional space with other peoples' stories is, for them, not so much a way of speaking for others but rather of carrying for them 'the pain they didn't choose' (Louis & Taïa, 2018), and thereby resisting the imperative to testimony imposed on victims of trauma. Carrying the pain of others means inviting them into the autofictional space without subsuming them in a transpersonal collective based on sameness: a high-stakes operation that can be managed in a range of ways. After surveying the most frequent ones through representative examples from this Element's corpus, I will compare Édouard Louis's novel *History of Violence*, which grapples with the author's experience of sexual assault, with Ostermeier's 2018 Schaubühne adaptation,[36] to explore the link between staging others and the political project of reclaiming narrative from its less emancipatory uses to, on one's own terms, 'tell otherwise'.

A variety of devices can be employed to represent others *as other* in the autofictional space: they can be omitted entirely or played by an actor; their words recounted as accurately as possible, invented, or reimagined. At one pole of the spectrum is dramatic ellipsis, exemplified by Selina Thompson when she refuses to name her collaborator, who abandoned the *salt.* project early.

---

[36] *Im Herzen der Gewalt* ('In the Heart of Violence'), co-produced with Paris's Théâtre de la Ville, Théâtre National Wallonie-Bruxelles, and St. Ann's Warehouse Brooklyn. The production has toured internationally with the novel's English title, *History of Violence*.

Thompson recounts how she did not 'think about the risk [the trip] might put them at, and in not naming them now, and not speaking to tell their story on their behalf, I'm trying not to repeat that harm' (Thompson, 2018: 23). Thompson's omission is framed as an ethical choice, in contrast with Louis's and Taïa's understanding of telling others' stories as a means of carrying their pain.

Alternatively, 'others' may be staged using words or props only: made present, in short, through their absence, as illustrated by *Who Killed My Father*. On stage, Louis reflects on what he knows about his father, addressing him in the second person in the form of an empty armchair, on which he then sits, in an embodied act of empathy after many years of resentment. His father is made visible also in a series of plastic model organs: a synecdochic evocation of his tortured body. These are pinned on a washing line alongside photographs of the politicians responsible for the inhumane policies that have caused his physical demise (see Figure 3). The full names and faces of the ministers, punctuated by the question, 'why do we never name these names in biographies?', contrast on stage with Louis's father's namelessness, which

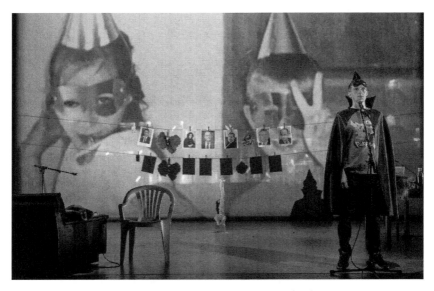

Figure 3 In his Pokémon T-shirt, Louis hangs plastic organs next to photographs of the politicians responsible for his father's physical demise, with a photograph of his childhood self projected behind him in *Qui a tué mon père* at the Schaubühne (Jean-Louis Fernandez/*Qui a tué mon père* (Schaubühne, dir. Thomas Ostermeier, produced by Schaubühne, Berlin and Théâtre de la Ville, Paris)).

at once reflects his disenfranchisement and signifies a withdrawal of accusation: it is not his father but the political elites that Louis names and shames, in this auto/allo-fiction[37] of a man who did not make history.

Inspired by Louis, *The Silence* also pivots around an absent father, who is, however, further subsumed into the autofictional self: less talked *about* or *to*, as Louis does, than occasionally imitated by the same actor playing Richter, as though Richter himself were impersonating his father. Recently deceased, Richter's father is doubly absent, the play's fictionalised un-silencing possible only without him. Louis's and Richter's fathers are thus presented through their absence as vulnerable and excluded: people who, unlike their sons, cannot and would not be present in the theatre space. The same vulnerability marks the para-dramatic presence of an 'other' in Cash Carraway's *Refuge Woman* (2018): billed as 'semi-autobiographical' (McClenaghan, 2018) and as 'Live Poverty Porn',[38] directed by Conrad Murray, and co-produced by the Battersea Arts Centre. Carraway's daughter, Annie – oft evoked in the play's account of the playwright's time living in women's refuges to escape an abusive relationship – is absent on stage but present in the auditorium, selling scripts for the production in the lobby then sitting with the audience in the front row. For Beswick, Annie's presence at a show based on the many traumatic experiences she has shared with her mother

> was most likely a practical decision (in that there was nobody Carraway could have asked to care for her child on that evening); however, Carraway did not opt to keep the child out of view as she might have done – hidden in the green room adjacent to the stage, occupied with a book, tablet, or smartphone. [. . .] Making her child highly visible before and during the performance, and involving her in the labour of the show, then, can be understood as a choice; it is one that served not only to solidify the horror and human impact of the stories Carraway shared on stage [. . .] but that also acted as a means of rendering visible the labours of motherhood in general, and single motherhood in particular, which often remain concealed from public view, relegated to the private, domestic realm. (Beswick, 2020: 95)

As well as making visible the relentless work of child-rearing for those financially unable to outsource it, Annie's presence invites questioning from spectators in ways that mirror, from an ethical standpoint, the 'meta-hermeneutic state of higher reflexiveness' (Iversen, 2020: 559) catalysed by autofiction at large. The experience of sitting in a room watching a child witness the retelling of their own and their mother's harrowing experiences may well raise questions or cause concern. The knee-jerk reaction of wanting to spare Annie this experience,

---

[37] The opposite of 'auto-', 'allo-' indicates alterity. I use it to indicate autofiction that focuses on the stories of others.

[38] See footnote 30.

relegating her to the green room mentioned by Beswick, confronts whoever might feel it with the paradox of similar scruples. To judge Carraway's decision to expose her daughter to the production is to reproduce the common practice of blaming mothers for societal shortcomings, as though the narration of hardship were what would cause trauma, rather than the hardship itself. The fact that the latter happens out of sight, unlike the child's presence in the theatre, exposes the moral hypocrisy of the imagined middle-class spectator, untouched by anything they can shut off and thus not feel complicit in.

The evocation of others through their absence (e.g., in Louis) or their para-dramatic presence (e.g., in Carraway) sits somewhere between the two poles of dramatic ellipsis (e.g., in Thompson) and the representation of a real-world other as an independent dramatic character by an actor, as in Debris Stevenson's *Poet in da Corner*, which premiered at the Royal Court in 2018 and pivots around the disruption, on the part of an 'other', of the autofictional self-narration. Advertised by the theatre as 'semi-autobiographical', the play mixes dance, grime music,[39] spoken word, and narration to tell the story of how grime allowed Stevenson to escape her working-class, Mormon background. Stevenson plays herself on stage, juxtaposing her story with the story of grime to narrate their parallel ascent from social deprivation to creative and commercial success. We learn how, thanks to her schoolmate, Saw Scaled Vyper, who introduced her to grime and whom she left behind in her social ascent, Stevenson found a language to express herself and her queer sexuality, becoming a poet, performer, and educator.

The play's ethical and political awkwardness agglomerates around Vyper. In performance, Stevenson's self-narration is interrupted by an actor playing Vyper, who bursts into the balcony and halts the show, accusing Stevenson of appropriating his story in an environment from which he remains structurally excluded. With Vyper's interruption, the play swerves from the (broadly speaking) factual into the fictional as the two face off on stage. The issues debated are thorny: Vyper is black, Stevenson is white; Stevenson is playing herself, Vyper is being discussed in his absence; while grime music – a counter-cultural, black genre – is being introduced into an affluent, West-London theatre by a white woman. Stevenson attempts to justify her decision while also signalling awareness of the compromises it entails, using the fictionalised Vyper to pre-empt and respond to accusations of bad practice. The play ends with Stevenson ceding the microphone to Vyper, who is officially included in the production, 'given a voice', and allowed to deliver a properly 'authentic' account of the story of grime.

The contrast between Stevenson playing herself and Jammz playing Vyper is stark and bespeaks some of the more controversial issues undergirding a production

---

[39] A musical genre that emerged in London in the 2000s.

like this one. Capitalising on grime's 'authenticity' in an overwhelmingly white space of middle-class cultural consumption, the telling of real Vyper's story, alongside his fictionalised appearance on stage, draws on the kind of 'authenticity by proxy' at work in *Superhoe*. Set against the play's own politicised ambitions as an 'inclusion story' – as I return to in Section 4 – Stevenson's decision to resolve the ethical and political impasse identified metatheatrically in performance by offering her (fictionalised) friend the (fictional) chance to speak for himself comes across, ultimately, as somewhat glib.

Despite its unconvincing resolution, *Poet in da Corner* makes the fictional nature of Vyper's presence obvious through his metatheatrical engagement with the performance, which he disrupts and critiques. Stevenson's production thus draws clear lines between the (at least partly) factual account of Vyper's past, bound up with Stevenson's self-narration, and the present of the production, which is clearly fictional. While similar distinctions are made in *History of Violence*'s source text, many are lost in Ostermeier's adaptation, to which the rest of this section attends, mirroring the broader scope of the discussion of *The Writer*. Comparing the adaptation to the source text, I shed light on the crucial role the choices made in representing others play in shaping and/or detracting from autofiction's political ambitions.

History of Violence tells the story of the assault Louis experienced during a spontaneous hook-up with a stranger, Reda, who stole from, pulled a gun on, and then raped him. Like much autofiction, it was written in the aftermath of trauma and can thus 'be seen as a means of situating the self in a new context when other relational constructs have been removed or jeopardized' (Dix, 2018: 4): a form, in other words, of self-refashioning. In performance, the attack is recounted by the author/narrator, played by actor Laurenz Laufenberg, to the audience and to a grotesque host of characters: judgemental police officers, bored doctors, and Louis's working-class sister Clara. Complementing these attempts to verbalise his experience is Louis's running commentary, delivered by Laufenberg, on the failures thereof. Blown up on live camera or speaking through microphones, other cast members embody Édouard's dissociation, becoming, in turn, a voice in his head or parts of a body from which he feels estranged, as he does, before long, from his story. Forced into the mould of police reports, misconstrued, used by his working-class relatives as confirmation of his out-of-touch snobbery, and weaponised for racist intents, the story of his assault elicits not empathy but censorship and insinuations. The police gloat in describing his aggressor, who is Kabyle (thus ethnically Berber), as 'Arab', while the confused, post-traumatic feelings the protagonist shares with his sister are relayed mockingly by Clara to her husband, as a mortified Édouard listens behind the door, correcting her retelling of his story.

The production's multimedia and meta-narrative layers – Laufenberg alternates between re-enacting Édouard's experiences, narrating them, and commenting on his own and others' attempts to do so – which blend with each other in performance in surreal narrative metalepsis, dramatise the narrative stranglehold of the aftermath of trauma: the imperative to tell, retell, and conform to the tropes of victimhood imposed on the fissured self. These devices reproduce literary tense shifts on stage, 'emphasis[ing] the chronological and ontological separation of event and narration' (Schmitt, 2022: 93–94). They serve to pick apart the artifice of self-storytelling, from the tears one conjures to concretise pain to the scripts that make trauma intelligible. Structuring each exchange and shoring up a justice system that counters violence with violence and robs one of one's story – 'it's no longer up to you, sir, this belongs to the law now', the police officer tells Édouard, when he wants to withdraw his deposition – are the neat categories of victim and perpetrator. Wordless, tender, the live selfie-videos of the two men in bed, just minutes before the attack, offer glimpses of the ambiguity these labels gloss over. The performance does not shy away from staging the act at the heart of the story. We see the gun, the insults, the rape itself: codified forms of violence we can recognise and name. What haunts the text and production, however, and their forensic examination of a single event is a less visible network of violence: the longue durée of trauma, in which victims and perpetrators merge. Legacies of racism, class oppression, and homophobia are played out on stage, in the postcolonial encounter between Reda and Édouard, and in the rift between Édouard, a 'class defector', and his left-behind sister.

History of Violence shares the characteristic objectives, identified by Heddon (2008: 31), of politicised autobiography on stage: '(i) to use personal experience in order to render visible oppression and inequality; (ii) to render simultaneously such experiences historically contingent (and therefore possible to change); (iii) to deny any simple referentiality between a life and its representation while acknowledging that representation is itself a discursive technology'. The oppression grappled with, however, is not principally his own; arguably more important to Louis's political project are the story's 'others': Clara and Reda, and the ambivalent role of each in imbricated histories of colonial, racial, classed, sexual, and gendered violence. It is in the dramatic representation of these two, crucial 'others' that Louis's political project takes shape, with all its potential and pitfalls.

Reda, a second-generation immigrant, is initially portrayed as a seductive and playful bad boy. Uninterested in Édouard's shows of intellectualism, he hits on him in the street at night, offering him weed, then asking to be invited back to his, to which Édouard concedes. Before things take a turn for the worse, in what Louis frames a posteriori as an explosion of shame, poverty, and internalised homophobia, the two have sex and talk about Reda's history. In the novel, this account, which follows Reda's father's journey from Northern Algeria to France twenty years before Reda's birth, is heavily mediated by the autofictional 'I'. The backbone of what are presented as the real events Reda tells Édouard becomes a springboard for acts of narrative empathy, which are marked as such in the text. Reda's and his father's stories thus become the 'site of a local fictionalization within a globally factual narrative' (James, 2022: 54), through what Schaeffer (2010: 219) might call a 'ludic feint of mental acts' on the part of the author/protagonist. Through phrases like '*I have no doubt* he feared the future less than he feared the past' and '*maybe* it was raining' (Louis, 2018: 69, emphasis mine), it becomes clear that Édouard is fictionally expanding on what he has heard, projecting his own experiences onto Reda's father, whom he relates to as a kindred soul.

> I told Clara [Reda's] father must always have dreamed of leaving, of running away. [. . .] Maybe, I told her, he wanted to go to a place where he had no friends, no family, no past; that's how I felt the first time I left for the city, and I can't be the only one. [. . .] Clara listened as I made my speculations, and chimed in with her own. By leaving, I said, he must have thought he could get rid of his past, that with no past, no history, and thus no shame, he could try on all the styles and poses we secretly want to try but deny ourselves. [. . .] Reda said his father came here to make money, but that doesn't prove anything one way or another. (Louis, 2018: 67–68)

Here as in the rest of the text, the narrative is layered and polyphonic. A story we are told is factual is recounted, augmented, and reimagined by a range of narrators: first told by Reda's father to his son, it is repeated by Reda to Édouard, then – in a further fictionalised version – by Édouard to Clara and, simultaneously, to the reader/spectator. In imagining/writing it, the author/narrator even draws on his own past – to give faces to its characters, for example – while acknowledging he is doing so. This narrative mediation goes even further than Faye's in Cusk's trilogy, signalling that not only the story's style and tone but also its content is co-authored. The 'enunciative gap' of each 'I' is thus inhabited chorally by a range of other 'I's, modelling within the text the invitation extended by autofiction. This intersubjective fictionalisation of Reda's origin story bespeaks Louis's commitment to humanising his assailant, who is reduced by the police to a type, a statistic: 'most of the robberies we see ... they're usually committed by foreigners, by Arabs', the officer tells Édouard, gloating (111).

The attempt to give texture to Reda's story resonates with the 'series of interconnected spheres' methodology explored, in the realm of applied story-telling, by Sujatha Fernandes.[40] Building on multi-sited ethnography's aim of

---

[40] Presented as a work in progress at the 2023 Narrative Matters conference in Tampere and referenced with the author's permission.

mapping interrelated processes in the world system to represent complex phenomena, Fernandes's methodology seeks to eschew the unsystematic and hyper-individualised thinking encouraged by neoliberal logics and inherent as a risk in storytelling – particularly when it focuses, as it most often does, on a single protagonist. In its place is the attempt to map interconnectedness – in line, for example, with the circulation of capital – by telling a range of overlapping or tangent stories with (a) different protagonist(s), at once complexifying our understanding of enmeshed phenomena *and* deploying the affective hold and empathy-eliciting properties of narrative form. Akin to Fernandes's work, Louis's writing can be seen to resist the kind of co-option to which stories like this one – under the label of 'trauma porn' – tend to be subjected.

Ostermeier's production is skilful in dramatising the text's narrative layers. Through live camera, microphones, fluid alternation between mimetic re-enactment and diegetic commentary and meta-commentary, the production conveys the text's focus not on events but on the stakes of their narrativisation. It is thus all the more striking that, in representing Reda's story – a crucial moment in the text's political project – these markers of mediation are, if not dropped, at least heavily reduced. In the role of Reda, Renato Schuch tells the entire story himself, incorporating what, in the novel, are marked as clearly fictionalised details and projections added by Édouard. A surreal atmosphere permeates the scene: Reda, who we are told was a troublemaker and left school early, is suddenly gifted with remarkable fluency, speaking in a voice closer to the author/protagonist's than to what we have heard thus far of his own, to which he returns soon after, when he segues into anti-Arab, racist slurs. As Schuch talks, Laufenberg gets out of bed and stares dreamily at images of the landscapes Reda's father must have crossed projected behind them, then begins to write and draw, tracing the story's geographies on a map of Paris (see Figure 4). The staging of his act of imaginative empathy is thus displaced from the crucial arena of narrative to a far more subtle act of illustration.

The choice to dispense with or at least significantly tone down the dramatic devices signalling narrative mediation in this scene, reducing them to the jarring nature of Reda's sudden eloquence, is at odds with the political project of Louis's autofictional narrative. Instead of foregrounding Louis's fictionalisation of Reda's story as a means to humanise his aggressor, complicate his own victim position, and situate himself alongside Reda in the titular history of violence, Schuch/Reda's articulate rendering of his own story elevates him, dramatically, out of the role of the undereducated immigrant and makes the act of understanding invited by the play feel dependent on his own sophisticated articulation of his postcolonial plight, presented, by and large, as simply a true story.

Figure 4 Reda (Schuch) tells his father's story while Édouard (Laufenberg) traces its geographies on a map of Paris in *History of Violence* at the Schaubühne (Arno Declair/*Im Herzen der Gewalt* (Schaubühne, dir. Thomas Ostermeier, produced by Schaubühne, Berlin; Théâtre de la Ville, Paris; Théâtre National Wallonie-Bruxelles and St. Ann's Warehouse, Brooklyn)).

Similar problems undergird the staging of Clara, as the novel's attempt to understand the (fictionalised version of the) author's sister and her classed suffering also loses nuance on stage. Uncomprehending and judgemental, her breasts revealed almost entirely by a low-cut, leopard-skin top and stuck out comically to communicate disapproval, actor Alina Stiegler seems to embody the bourgeois fantasy of a working-class woman. This caricatured performance accentuates her less palatable views, inviting laughter from a position of superiority. She has no patience with her brother's attempt to empathise with Reda as a marginalised, socially abject other, or to see his theft as 'logical', and even accuses Édouard of faking his homosexuality to provoke the rejection of a family he despises. While these ideas are presented in the novel – working through layers of alienation, resentment, and frustration – as symptomatic of the network of violence Clara, too, is enmeshed in and a victim of, this work is compromised on stage in favour of some comic relief.

When her husband makes a bad-taste joke, Clara looks into the audience and shrugs, admitting 'this is our humour'. The 'our' stands not only for Louis's family but for the working class at large, represented on stage by two other characters played by the same actor, Christoph Gawenda, renowned for his slapstick performances: Clara's husband and the siblings' mother. Gawenda renders Clara's husband as an unfeeling, beer-drinking quasi-primate, and the siblings' mother in hysterical drag, as s/he recounts – with jarringly clownish exaggeration – what are actually harrowing tales of care work, scatologically emphasised on stage to the point of ridicule. Her subsequent reappearance only detracts further from any possible compassion, as she voices bigoted views while sweeping the floor and pantomime-sobbing through exaggerated makeup. The audience's vocal amusement on the evenings I attended was mirrored in reviews: while Gawenda's performance may be slightly heavy handed, writes Barbara Behrendt for *Deutschlandfunk Kultur* (2018, my translation), 'at least this ensures a few lighter moments in what is not exactly a cheerful evening'. That these 'lighter moments' are achieved through grotesque stereotyping of real, working-class people is not remarked upon, in its wholesale contradiction of the text's attempts to humanise and understand beyond facile forms of othering.

The text and play end on a controversial offering in post-truth times. When violence is thrust upon us, the author/protagonist explains, we have one residual form of agency: denial through lies. If the body bears the undeniable traces of trauma, the only space of freedom at one's disposal is one's story. And indeed, Édouard reflects, lying has saved him already, allowing him to escape his violent and homophobic milieu by reinventing himself; it has helped him 'resist a truth that was forced on me, on my tissues, on my organs – a truth that was already rooted inside me, that had been rooted inside me for a long time, but that had been planted there by others, that came from without' (219). This wrestling back of narrative as a self-fashioning lie is identified here as autofiction's fundamental impetus. 'Telling otherwise' to *become other* is, for Louis, a concretisation of Hannah Arendt's radical conception of lying, which Louis cites on page and stage:

> Arendt writes: 'In other words, the deliberate denial of factual truth – the ability to lie – and the capacity to change facts – the ability to act – are interconnected; they owe their existence to the same source: imagination. It is by no means a matter of course that we can say, "The sun shines", when it actually is raining . . . ; rather, it indicates that while we are well equipped for the world, sensually as well as mentally, we are not fitted or embedded into it as one of its inalienable parts. We are free to change the world and to start something new in it.' That's what saved me – my ability to deny the facts. (Louis, 2018: 220)

By foregrounding the work of narrative in the encounter between self and other – both its humanising potential, in imagining Reda's story, and its normative violence, in the forensic interrogations – the play returns to the scene of trauma to tell it again, but to tell it otherwise, in the hope of becoming, through what Arendt calls one's 'ability to deny the facts', 'something other than what the world has made of us' (Louis & Taïa, 2018). Rejecting the scripts superimposed on his experience, Louis draws on it not to give testimony but to harness it to his political project of radical empathy. Through forensic examination of a violent encounter and its aftermath, and the autofictional rewriting thereof, violence is de-individualised and returned to its structural dimension, undercutting facile processes of othering. Into these, unfortunately, the production on occasion falls, by privileging tropes of bourgeois theatre over attention to the text's handling of fictionalised lived experience.

This section has reflected on ways of representing the autofictional self, alongside and in contrast to others. Akin to fact/fiction, the distinction between self and other forms, in theatres of autofiction, its own kind of continuum, with one feeding into and shaping the other. Decisive, however, in parsing the referential difference between autofictional selves and 'others' – namely, between who is actually speaking and who is being spoken for – are the logics of inclusion and exclusion governing the theatrical space that will be addressed in the next and final section.

4 Inclusion/Exclusion

Wagner-Egelhaaf (2022: 30) proposes that, as '[a]utofiction produces real-life effects' on the life described, it should be understood as 'fundamentally performative'. She is referring here to literary autofiction, in which – as we have seen – 'the performative text/life relation' forms a 'Möbius strip' (31). Yet the act of writing happens in private, and the reader is left with its traces, to be pieced together with what is communicated about its consequences, paratextually and/or contextually: the fallout on the author's personal life, divorces, deaths.[41] Theatres of autofiction, on the other hand, unfold in real time: the work is created and received simultaneously in a live Möbius strip, particularly when authors perform themselves. Not only do they transgress '*textual* borders by turning what Genette referred to as the paratextual threshold (that mediates between experience and the text) into the experience itself' (Iversen, 2020: 559, emphasis original), they do so live in a collective setting. If the author is on stage, the lives of author and spectator even coincide with the autofictional act for the latter's duration.

Considering their *doubly* performative dimension (as performances that, in turn, make things happen), and the comparatively broader representation of marginalised voices therein – indeed, as seen in the Introduction, the

---

[41] Wagner-Egelhaaf refers to Doubrovsky's *Le livre brisé* (1989), written in collaboration with his wife, who committed suicide during the writing process. See also Knausgaard on the effects of his work (2016).

autofictional literary canon is not particularly diverse – theatres of autofiction are a privileged place to interrogate the logics of inclusion and exclusion regulating the cultural sphere, negotiated, on stage and in auditoria, physically and in real time. The fault lines between who can self-fictionalise and who features only as an 'other', concretised in the theatre, shed light on the conditions of access to the creative industries and on the role of autofiction in validating or resisting them.

This section considers two phenomena – the popularity of 'autosociobiographical' plays at Berlin's Schaubühne, and of the creative industries' 'rags to riches' story on British stages – to interrogate these conditions of access comparatively. It probes the potential and pitfalls of each narrative trope, or rather, as I propose, of each 'inclusion paradigm': the European 'scholarship boy' and the British 'Billy Elliot paradigm'. To do so, I focus on marginalisation related to class: the central preoccupation of social mobility stories. Class tends to be the sticking point of inclusion initiatives in academic and cultural institutions, since, as Rita Felski (2000: 42) points out, it 'does not have the same status as race or gender in debates over equal representations [...] simply because [academic and para-academic] culture inescapably alters the class identities of those who inhabit it'. With this in mind, I look at autofictional social mobility stories on stage, asking on what conditions their aesthetics of inclusion risk becoming, to adapt Sarah Ahmed (2012: 34) on race, about 'changing perceptions' of bourgeois culture rather than changing its organisations.

4.1 Uplift through Education

The previous sections' discussion of *Returning to Reims*, *Who Killed My Father*, and *History of Violence* revealed a number of shared features, on page and stage alike: an autofictional narrator with lived experience of social mobility, who testifies to the processes of self-transformation (or *autopoiesis*) involved; a focus on the act of transgressing the frontier between classes, which is revisited through memory and narration or physically re-enacted, as in Eribon's titular return home; and a sociologically motivated interest in class and classed violence (see Twellmann & Lammers, 2023). These traits characterise a corpus of works that has garnered much scholarly and critical attention, particularly in Germany, since the astonishing success of *Returning to Reims*'s German translation in 2016 (see Kargl & Terrisse, 2020). Gathered under the label of 'autosociobiography' – coined by Ernaux (2003) with reference to her own prose and repurposed in German scholarship (see Twellmann & Lammers: 64) – this newly theorised genre can be understood as a subcategory of what

Anglo-American literary scholars refer to as autotheory: a term used since the 2010s to indicate hybrid blends of autobiography or memoir and philosophy or critical theory (see Fournier, 2022). Autosociobiography spans the work of the upwardly mobile authors who directly or indirectly inspired Eribon's socio-logically informed self-narration – for example, Bourdieu, Ernaux, and Richard Hoggart – and the work of those inspired *by* Eribon, such as his friend and mentee Louis.

Defined as a 'combination of autofictional narration and sociological diagno-sis' (Hiden, 2020: 105, my translation), autosociobiography's literary success has had far-reaching echoes. In Germany, it kick-started a dormant conversation about classism, revivifying a conceptual apparatus that had been all but ban-ished, alongside Marxist politics, with the fall of the Berlin wall (see Twellmann & Lammers, 2023: 53). Theatre houses, on the other hand, have responded with stage adaptations, led by Berlin's Schaubühne – the first and most system-atic to do so – under Ostermeier's artistic direction and in partnership with other mainstage, international institutions. The Schaubühne is not alone in its interest in these texts: other high-profile venues that have produced or programmed adaptations of Louis's, Eribon's, and Ernaux's work in recent years include Internationaal Theater Amsterdam, the Edinburgh International Festival, London's Young Vic and Almeida Theatre, the Berliner Ensemble, and Munich's Residenztheater and Kammerspiele. However, as its adaptations were developed in direct collaboration with Louis and Eribon, the Schaubühne constitutes a particularly insightful theatre of autofiction.

The popularity of these works is symptomatic of a renewed interest, across national borders, in cultural representations of class and social mobility grounded in lived experience. This section interrogates this phenomenon and its reception, probing what it reveals about the role of theatres of autofiction in negotiating, amplifying, and/or neutering class struggles in the cultural sphere. To this end, it offers a contextualised reading of Ostermeier's adaptations of *Returning to Reims*, *Who Killed My Father*, and *History of Violence*, exploring how the autofictional source material is put to work in the Schaubühne auditor-ium. It complicates the dominant reading of these productions as reflecting on logics of exclusion with the aim of exposing the liberal left's neglect of working-class communities, and thus the part it has played in facilitating the rise of the far right among them. I argue instead that, drawing on autofictional material, these productions represent forms of class-, sexuality-, and ethnicity-based exclusion – both suffered and perpetrated by the working classes – from a position of assimilation into the audience's milieu, establishing a classed bond between the imagined (bourgeois) spectator and the author-character. On the one hand, this locates exclusion outside the theatre: be it in working-class homophobia or in the violence of austerity politics. On the other, by joining in condemning the forms of exclusion portrayed and welcoming the socially mobile author-character, audiences can be reassured of the inclusiveness of bourgeois culture.

Reviewers and creative teams alike have located the political value of these productions in their preoccupation with the socio-political disenfranchisement of the formerly socialist working classes, in connection with the global rise of the populist right (see Zarin, 2018; Haydon, 2017). This Element began with a quote from Nina Hoss on the political urgency of adapting Eribon in response to Trump's presidency: the project thus emerged, in direct opposition to fictional works, out of Hoss's and Ostermeier's desire to shed light on the liberal left's contribution, through its neglect of the working classes, to the crises of our times (see Zarin, 2018). Louis articulates his political project along similar lines. Harbouring no illusions about the make-up of his audiences, he talks of making theatre 'for and against the bourgeoisie; for my enemies', to expose them to 'the things the audience don't want to be confronted with'.[42] He wants his 'art to make people feel bad', 'uncomfortable': 'to confront you with what you are not doing'.[43]

According to this dominant account, it is the workings of socio-political *exclusion* – illuminated by the autofictional exploration of the authors' milieus of origin – that constitute the works' core political material: what Louis calls 'the things the audience don't want to be confronted with'. This is reinforced by the fact that working-class exclusion is reflected (on) from the vantage point of a further exclusion: ostracised by their communities due to their homosexuality, both Eribon and Louis speak from a position of twofold marginalisation, the second allowing them, ultimately, to overcome the first through upward social mobility. Indeed, it is the exclusion they suffer due to their sexuality that instils in them the desire to evade a community they were never allowed to belong to and to reject the ideals of masculinity enforced in it, which involve – among other things – defying authority, quitting school as early as possible, and joining the factory workforce. Investing in their education thus offers them alternative role models and a way out.

While exclusion narratives are certainly a common feature of autosociobiography, it is another recurring narrative, I suggest, that is equally if not more pivotal to the success of these productions. Shoring up their attempt to evoke and understand absent people, places, and things is a potent story of inclusion,

---

[42] Statements made during an online Q&A organised by the Oxford University Queer Intersections Network.

[43] See Louis and Ken Loach in conversation on *Al Jazeera*, www.youtube.com/watch?v=J89RTrx1_eM&ab_channel=AlJazeeraEnglish (22:53–23:50).

affectively dominant in the theatre space. This allows theatregoers to at once entertain the flattering notion of grappling with (their responsibilities in) political exclusion *and* enjoy an affectively rewarding inclusion story.

To trace how this inclusion story operates on stage and in the auditorium, I consider the type of 'invitation' it extends in its institutional context. Following Liz Tomlin (2019: 35),

> Gareth White's (2013) notion of the invitation that is made to the spectator, and the importance of the aesthetic design of the invitation to its ultimate efficacy, will be appropriated [. . .] as a useful lens through which intention and efficacy in the projects of political theatres might be examined. [. . . T]he political artist can design their invitation in ways that are more or less likely to affect the spectator, more or less likely to inspire the spectator to take up the invitation to play their part, however small, in furthering political change.

Attending to the aesthetic design of the productions' 'invitation' complicates dominant interpretations of the cultural and political work they do in their material context, avoiding reductive or complacent readings. A similar approach might be fruitfully applied to other adaptations of autofictional material, particularly those centred on experiences of marginalisation.

At stake, here, is not so much the *real* audience but the imagined spectator conjured and targeted by Schaubühne productions, which can be reconstructed textually and contextually. Surrounded by luxury boutiques in West Berlin's wealthy district of Charlottenburg, the Schaubühne hosts an affluent, liberal audience whose habitus is a popular leitmotiv of its repertoire productions. In-jokes referencing either *topoi* of bourgeois Berliner lifestyle or other Schaubühne productions pepper the repertoire, rewarding intertextual familiarity with the programme and ensemble – including the actors' previous roles and real-world biographies – and cultivating a sense of exclusivity. As artistic director, Ostermeier is as clear as Louis about whom he caters to. Commenting on the dominance of the canon in his programming, he explains its function as a 'Trojan horse':

> It's as simple as that. You write on the tin *An Enemy of the People*, *Hedda Gabler* or *Hamlet*, and you cater to the audience, from MOMA in New York to the Tate Modern in London, or the Gropius-Bau here in Berlin. That is why after the era of postmodernism we have recently seen the return of culture and of *Bildung*. I have the feeling that once again it is expected that you know what a symphony is, that you know your stuff about art history and also about the literary classics. And so people come to pick up this knowledge in the theatre; they say, I won't manage to read *Hamlet*, but if Ostermeier does it at the Schaubühne, then I go and watch it, so I know what it is about because I might need to know at some point. So I imply people get their dose of the classical literary canon to fill their knowledge gaps,

and I then show them the classics as if they were a contemporary play. (Bönisch & Ostermeier, 2016: 608–609)

Products and advocates of a highbrow understanding of culture and *Bildung*, or education, Ostermeier's imagined audience – the slice of society who feel a responsibility to engage with the classics – is lured into attendance through the promise of a crash-course in the canon, into which something 'relevant' to the contemporary world is interwoven. Ostermeier has no qualms in identifying the theatre as a fundamentally bourgeois space: a socially uniform arena, whose politicisation involves feeding the initiated unexpected morsels. Fittingly, while the autosociobiographical texts in question are not classics, they bear the seal of highbrow approval. Imports from the idealised scene of French theory – Eribon studied with Bourdieu, before mentoring Louis – and distributed by prestigious German publishing houses, they offer a heavily mediated thus somewhat rarefied approach to their (locally relevant) political concerns, tailored to the same imagined spectator.

A twofold 'invitation' is thus proffered by the productions: to join in with a celebration first of highbrow culture, then of a set of values presented as unanimously shared in the theatre space. Indeed, the seductive fantasy that highbrow European culture is in itself a progressive social force is implicit in the stories told. These are, for better or for worse, tales of social ascent through education and consequent gains in cultural capital that champion the 'scholarship boy' inclusion paradigm. I use Hoggart's (1957) term metaphorically (as education in France and Germany is free at the point of use), to indicate the paradigmatic success story of the working-class high achiever, saved by the levelling powers of education, which grants access to a world demanding of them a radical self-refashioning. And indeed, both writers' stories begin in a state of exclusion and undernourished intelligence: victims of homophobic violence in their working-class milieus, they harness their intellectual curiosity to 'make it out'. For all their reflections on its classed potential to exclude, school becomes a refuge and opportunity: through exposure to literature, philosophy, and the arts, they learn their own worth, develop critical capacities, and gain access to the elite institutions of French higher education. Both are high achievers who, through hard work and determination, ascend into the intellectual bourgeoisie, from the midst of which – and, crucially, *to* which – they speak of the exclusion they have evaded, linked to poverty, class oppression, and homophobia.

The inclusion paradigm's affective pull is reinforced by the aesthetic design of the production's 'invitation'. *Returning to Reims*'s video footage, for example, features curated shots of grown-up Eribon in a Parisian bookshop, flicking sensually through a Derrida text. Shortly afterwards, the cement block he called home as a child – described in (his own) harsh terms by the voice-over – is juxtaposed with a sumptuous image of Paris's Opéra Garnier: a 'temple of culture', as Delphine Edy (2020: 99, my translation) refers to it in an analysis of the production. The building is filmed first from the outside, in all its intimidating glory, then – through aestheticising fragmentation – penetrated: glossy high heels ascending stairs; cocktail dresses glinting in the chandelier's candlelight; champagne bottles popping open; Eribon and his partner getting their tickets checked by a smiling usher, then ensconced in a private, velvet-coated box: a more glamorous version of the space in which the performance unfolds (see Figure 5). As the voice-over, reading from Eribon's text, muses on the learned nature of cultural appreciation – art, in short, is for the bourgeoisie – one is invited into a feeling of collective relief for having made it into such a shiny, sophisticated world. Identification is thus predicated, across classed divides, on a shared appreciation of these practices. Folarin describes something similar in Teju Cole's debut novel *Open City* (2011), where the protagonist's evocation of 'a dizzying number of Western artists and thinkers' and his

Figure 5 Video footage of Eribon gaining access to the Opéra in Paris is projected behind Redfern as she reads from Eribon's text in *Returning to Reims* at the Schaubühne (David Baltzer/bildbuehne.de/*Returning to Reims* (Schaubühne, dir. Thomas Ostermeier, produced by Schaubühne, Berlin; Manchester International Festival; HOME, Manchester and Théâtre de la Ville, Paris)).

'preference for classical radio stations from Canada, Germany, and the Netherlands' serves to facilitate identification across (potential) racial divides, signalling 'to the reader that Julius is immersed in Western high culture, and that Western readers are entering a safe, well-appointed space in which their admiration for these same figures will be affirmed.'

Not only shiny and sophisticated, the conjured world is also inclusive, liberal, and fair. Indeed, emphasised throughout is a bond of liberal solidarity between author-character and audience, united in condemning the social ills represented on stage, from working-class homophobia to austerity politics. The productions' 'invitation' is thus predicated on sameness: the audience is never challenged or made uncomfortable; rather, a set of values are performed as shared. By the same token, the mechanisms of social exclusion grappled with on stage are located firmly *outside* the auditorium, resulting in an affirmative affect in the theatre space. The theatre event itself is the most tangible proof of this, as the socially mobile hero literally takes centre stage, their inclusion into the intellectual bourgeoisie physically realised in the autopoietic feedback loop of performance (Fischer-Lichte, 2014).

This mirroring relationship between socially mobile author-character and bourgeois spectator affectively vouches, I argue, for the liberalising effect of bourgeois cultural practices themselves. Implied in the oft-marked distinction between those present and those absent, the includers and the excluders – and thus, by implication, the working class and the cultural elite – is the sense that participation in bourgeois culture fosters, over time, those same liberal values whose hegemonic presence in this microcosm is repeatedly affirmed. One is here, in other words, because one is inclusive, open-minded, and liberal, but also: one is inclusive, open-minded, and liberal because one is (used to being) here. This draws a sharp outline between the collective self in the theatre space and a collective other outside it, divided along a line of entitlement to the cultural practice at hand. Discussed in Section 2.1, the recurring dance sequences in *Who Killed My Father* illustrate this well. Harking back to Louis's father's shame at his son's camp mannerisms and his inability to watch the innocent performance, Louis's re-enactment of it on stage overwrites this painful memory. 'Look, dad', Louis repeats, staring into the audience, and those present – unlike his father – can and do.

This invitation to identificatory sameness undergirds the production from the outset. Sitting at his MacBook, Louis opens his monologue by citing prison abolitionist Ruth Wilson Gilmore, bringing an academic framework to bear on the traumatic experiences he then narrates and re-enacts. While his knowledge-worker millennial appearance, liberal values, and academic language feel close to the imagined audience's, his final indictment of the ruling classes, discussed in

Section 3.2, comes across as less close to home, particularly through the comfortable middle distance of international circulation, performed to an audience who overall have little to no say in French elections. Arguably dominant, then, is the figure of the 'class defector' who has made it out and speaks the language of the liberal middle classes, rather than the hard-hitting confrontation Louis aims for.

This signalling of sameness jars with other autofictional productions about working-class experience. The first monologue of Carraway's *Refuge Woman* (2018: 7), for example, features a list of places where the author-character stayed in women's refuges, after which Carraway looks into the audience to acknowledge that, to them, this is 'merely a list of mediocre places – where you *might* be able to afford a property'. While making similar assumptions to the Schaubühne adaptations about the make-up of the audience, Carraway's production establishes difference from the outset, exploits it dramaturgically, and sustains it throughout, marking off the play's authentic material as something that cannot be simply identified with. In the Schaubühne adaptations, by contrast, difference is exorcised almost entirely. The formerly working-class author-character is assimilated in their autopoietic, bourgeois identity, while the other working-class characters – or fictionalised real people – are either absent; represented mutely in video footage (Eribon's mum, protesting crowds, etc.); or performed as grotesque caricatures, further marking them out as 'other', at odds with the auditorium community, like Clara and her husband and mother in *History of Violence*, discussed in Section 3.2.

Through the aesthetic design of their 'invitations', the Schaubühne adaptations risk affectively endorsing the illusion of social mobility through access to culture and education as a solution to systemic oppression, if only for those with intellectual aptitude and determination. This reduces the working class to a community to be evaded, while singling out a certain type of individual as not only deserving but *able* to climb the social ladder – locating progressive politics, in other words, in heightening people's chances of moving 'up and out' rather than improving the 'absolute position of those at the bottom' (Swift, 2020). This jars, I argue, with both the source texts' reflections on, and Ostermeier's commitment to engaging with, the liberal left's desertion of the working class, which has left a gap the far right has been quick to fill (see Piketty, 2018). At a time of crisis for (state-subsidised) culture, the exploration of working-class exclusion in bourgeois echo chambers, in which the working class becomes a metaphor, a caricature, or an abstraction, present only in the testimony of a socially mobile escapee, risks further entrenching the logics of exclusion with which the productions purportedly grapple.

Having located exclusion firmly outside the theatre, we are left with what we might call, to riff on Fischer-Lichte's term (2014), an *autofictional* feedback loop among those present, who are collectively refashioned into an inclusive, open-minded audience.[44] The updated version of *Returning to Reims* reinforces this effect. Though intersectionality is brought into the picture, with two black actors (Nove and Redfern) sharing autofictional accounts of experiences of racism and marginalisation, sameness remains dominant in the performance's 'invitation', subsuming the potentially disruptive additional material. When calling out the forms of racism experienced in the theatre industry, for example, Redfern first expresses, with metatheatrical irony, how glad she is to 'not be in the theatre' anymore (the play is set in a film studio), where she was always the token black actor in the production or ensemble, forced to represent racialised characters or issues. This was greeted, on the nights I attended, with unbridled hilarity on the part of the prevalently white audience, despite it being an accurate description of widespread practices, not least at the Schaubühne. Redfern then makes clear – perhaps ironically, perhaps not – that the audience has no part to play in the problem. While self-proclaimed politicised theatre-makers, locked in their ivory tower, think canonical, leading roles should be played by white actors only or people will not be able to 'identify', the audience – Redfern reassures – is more open-minded: they may well all be middle-class graduates, but they are not so bigoted. While one can only hope this is true, what is affectively achieved is at once self-deprecating irony on the part of an institution that will only emerge strengthened by it (the Schaubühne, we are informed, is at least *aware* of its whiteness), and the defence of the audience as, once again, belonging to the most liberal, open-minded, and morally righteous segment of the population.

What Louis calls 'writing for his enemy', to confront them with the mechanisms of social exclusion in which they are complicit, risks becoming in these adaptations a nostalgic and exoticising celebration of the inclusive potential of highbrow European culture: be it French theory – evoked by the Derrida text Eribon so sensuously handles – or the transformative potential of access to education, through the 'scholarship boy' inclusion paradigm. This is, in turn, metatheatrically revealing of the theatre's understanding of its own social role as part of an apparatus of educational institutions, open and available to intellectually gifted and deserving 'scholarship boys'. The autofictional is capitalised on to reinforce this perception, harnessing its authenticating effects to a range of contradictory ends. This projected self-image differs quite substantially, as the next section details, from British theatre's performance of its social role and responsibilities, linked less to education, highbrow culture, and intellectual achievement, and more to a talent-driven, equalising, creative

---

[44] Audience response cannot, of course, be generalised, and this analysis is based on the evenings I attended.

industry ideal, as fostered by New Labour in the early 2000s and iconically embodied by Billy Elliott, the dancing protagonist of Stephen Daldry's box office hit (2000). In the UK, too, autofictional social mobility stories play a crucial role in sustaining this image.

4.2 Britain's Got Talent

Returning to Reims was co-produced with Manchester's HOME and the Manchester International Festival, and both *Who Killed My Father* and *The End of Eddy*, Louis's debut novel, have been adapted by and toured to a range of British venues, including London's Young Vic and the Edinburgh International Festival. And while Eribon and Louis have made something of a name for themselves in the UK, their critical acclaim has been a lot more modest there than in Germany. This, I suggest, is partly a result of the different resonance of the 'scholarship boy' inclusion paradigm. Despite being a British concept, the 'scholarship boy' is an arguably less invested collective myth in contemporary Britain than in continental Europe, and rightly so, as it is hard to make an even gestural case that the UK's education system, with its split in resourcing, prestige, and outcomes between state and private schools, and elite and non-elite institutions, is anything other than engineered to reproduce class divides (see Evans, 2023: 178–223). The exclusion mechanisms at work in educational institutions in France and Germany are comparatively more subtle, with schools and universities remaining free, state-subsidised, and on the surface merito-cratic. Without a belief in social mobility through education as an at least potentially intersubjective experience, the relatability of these works decreases.

The appeal of the 'scholarship boy' in contemporary Britain is prevalently nostalgic, as testified by the post-pandemic revival of Emlyn Williams's 1938 play *The Corn is Green* at the National Theatre. Described by Arifa Akbar (2022) in the *Guardian* as 'a kind of Billy Elliot of the Valleys', it tells the playwright's own social mobility story through the rags to riches tale of an illiterate teenager in a coal-mining town in nineteenth-century Wales, 'saved' by his English school teacher, who helps him secure a place at Oxford University. The play was marketed as 'semi-autobiographical', with the production emphasising its autofictionality through the presence on stage of an actor in the role of the playwright, busy fictionalising his own story. The darker aspects of the uplift through education plot are quickly dismissed – including the fate of Bessie, one of the teacher's 'failures', consigned to a life of service – in favour of 'the clear, simple narrative that Evans wants to better himself' (Akbar, 2022). 'Our hearts do soar and melt' writes Akbar, 'as the gifted Evans navigates his way towards a happy ending, and there are lovely, warm laughs along the way. This revival is a reminder that old stories, when they are good, stay that way, however riddled they are with nostalgia.' It is also a reminder of the affective pull of these paradigmatic plots, in which a resilient, gifted hero rises above their unequal lot. Coupled with Akbar's emotive review, the revival's place within the National Theatre's post-pandemic programming – at a time of great financial and emotional strain, newly visible inequality, and the lowest social mobility in over half a century (see van der Erve et al., 2023) – speaks volumes on its consolatory function in conjuring the mirage of a fairer society.

Akbar's term – 'a Billy Elliot of the Valleys' – is an interesting one, fusing as it does the two paradigms identified in this section. Despite Evans being arguably closer, in his intellectual aptitude and educational investment, to Louis and Eribon than to Billy Elliot, who discovers a talent and passion for ballet rather than reading, Akbar's choice reflects the young dancer's unparalleled status as British social mobility icon. And indeed, where autofiction and social mobility stories meet in British culture, it is often not intellectual pursuits but creative industry talent that they showcase. Oft cited in relevant scholarship as *the* example of Anglophone autosociobiography, Darren McGarvey's book *Poverty Safari: Understanding the Anger of Britain's Underclass* (2018) illustrates this well. Unlike his continental European counterparts, who tell similar stories to Eribon and Louis, McGarvey touches on many tropes of the social mobility plot, but with a fundamentally different tone and performance of authorship. The book begins with an account not of McGarvey's unusual love of books – a trope in French autosociobiography, signalling the ripeness for uplift through education of the soon-to-be 'scholarship boy' – but of his enduring struggles with reading. This does not stop him from making it as a rapper and going on to write a book, collaborate with the BBC, and become de facto middle class, but it signals a less radical break with his former milieu, alongside the non-intellectual catalyst of his and other British writers' social mobility journeys.

This is all the truer in the theatre industry, bespeaking the comparatively less highbrow[45] and more commercial status of theatre in British culture – compared to France and Germany, at least – as is confirmed, materially, by the respective funding structures. Writer and performer Scottee exemplifies what a social mobility journey like McGarvey's might look like in the theatre industry. In a previous version of his website's artist bio, he prides himself on being 'a multi-award winning, self taught artist with no formal education or

---

[45] This does not reflect the background of its gatekeepers and workers, who are almost exclusively middle class and Russell Group-educated, i.e., holding a degree from one of the most prestigious research universities in the UK (see Comunian et al., 2023).

qualifications': of having, in other words, made it alone, without refashioning himself through education and cultural training. Having worked for the BBC, in dance, opera, and photography, and having been 'commissioned by some of the UK's biggest cultural institutions' do not stop him from narrating how:

> I have been making shows, turns and theatre bollox since I was 14 and I accidentally came in contact with a bunch of theatrical types doing outreach on my estate.
>
> Soon after, I met Oliver Award Winning Duckie and got paid in fivers and chips, making short performances for drunk homosexuals in boozers and art institutes long before drag was about social mobility.
>
> I caught the attention of an audience and cut my teeth on small stages across the UK. Soon after I became Associate Artist at Roundhouse doing heavyweight light entertainment.[46]

'Theatre bollox' and 'theatre as *Bildung*' are, to put it mildly, quite some way from each other. Beyond its colourful phrasing, however, Scottee's bio exemplifies a social mobility plot popular in contemporary Britain. Scottee is 'saved' from his council estate not by school but by 'a bunch of theatrical types': it is the artistically talented that make it out of the working classes, through the social elevator of the creative industries that seeks out less the intellectually gifted in a traditional sense than gritty, 'authentic' voices. It is thus institutional 'outreach' rather than an individual's determination to assimilate into the cultural elite that drives social mobility. And indeed, since the turn of the millennium, the 'scholarship boy' has arguably been overtaken in the British social mobility imaginary by the ballet-dancing kid, the council estate footballer, the rapper who – like Conrad Murray – could have been in jail and is, instead, on stage or on *Top of the Pops*.

The shift from 'scholarship boy' to talent show star can be traced back to New Labour's investment in and rebranding of the creative industries in the early 2000s. Fuelling a conviction that, through Cool Britannia's[47] multifarious creative talent – from music to acting to dance – a new and more democratic avenue of social uplift would open, New Labour surfed the wave of the economic rise of the '90s to tell a seductive story. In the absence of an egalitarian education system, and speaking directly to an image of British culture as down-to-earth and authentic, the idea of harnessing a wide and joyous range of talent to forge a more equal society planted firm roots in mainstream political and cultural discourse (see Inchley, 2015). Recent autofictional social mobility stories on stage emerge from this imaginary, which has proved more resilient

---

[46] https://scottee.co.uk/

[47] Shorthand for the UK's economic rise during the 1990s and New Labour's project of reshaping the economy around the creative industries.

than the economic prosperity to which it was tied. With the creative industries replacing education as social mobility facilitators, inclusion becomes less bound up with highbrow culture – with philosophy and critical theory, but also with a bourgeois framing of theatre – and more a matter of mainstreaming counter-cultural activities: from 'boozers' populated by 'drunk homosexuals' to the BBC, in the case of Scottee; from hip-hop to political writing prizes, in the case of McGarvey.

We see this play out in *DenMarked* and *Poet in da Corner*. On the one hand, the two plays are comparable to the French works discussed in Section 4.1. Like them, both function autofictionally, both tell a social mobility story, and both are preoccupied with how the lived experience at their heart is illustrative of broader societal dynamics. In what is, as we have seen, a classically autosocio-biographical move, Stevenson even inscribes herself explicitly in a lineage of elective kinship by imitating a socially mobile predecessor: grime pioneer Dizzee Rascal, whose Mercury Prize-winning first album *Boy in da Corner* (2003) – like Eribon's work for Louis and his peers – offers Stevenson a blueprint, a role model, and permission to tell her story. On the other hand, British theatres of autosociobiography reveal significant differences. Rather than narratives of uplift through education, Stevenson and Murray map the journey of a counter-cultural form, drenched in suffering, anger, and social deprivation, from the margins into the mainstream; from the council estate into the theatre: grime for Stevenson, hip hop for Murray. In the wake of Dizzee Rascal – who grew up in a socially deprived environment, was expelled from school, then ended up a trailblazing millionaire with an OBE, even opening the 2012 London Olympics – Stevenson traces her own path from marginalisation to critical and commercial success, culminating on the Royal Court stage. Like McGarvey, Stevenson and Murray also struggle to read: Stevenson is dyslexic, finding freedom in the orality of lyrics, while Murray reflects, in the song 'No Books', on the lack of intellectual stimuli in his upbringing and on the intimi-datory, excluding aura of highbrow culture (Murray, 2022: 51–53).

Despite their different inclusion paradigms – the 'scholarship boys' make it because they are intellectually gifted, whereas the 'Billy Elliots' escape through creative talent – these autofictional stagings of social mobility stories, at the Schaubühne and Royal Court alike, elicit similar affective responses, offering precious insights into the role and responsibilities of theatre in each context's cultural imaginary. Discussed in Section 3.2, the ending of *Poet in da Corner* is an eloquent illustration of this, foregrounding the enmeshment of the three thematic nodes on which this Element has focused. The play's resolution, which sees Vyper, the story's excluded other, performatively included in the theatrical fiction, underwrites how autofiction's political stakes take shape in the imbricated negotiation of fact/fiction, self/other, and inclusion/exclusion. Similarly to *The Writer*, the ending signals the playwright's political intentions in their ideal form, alongside their inevitable failure. Unlike in *The Writer*, however, this failure is not acknowledged in the play's finale. Rather, *Poet in da Corner* provides a textual solution to its material concerns, in a move that remains largely unproblematised in the representational economy of the drama. Encouraging the audience to get up and join in with a raucous, simulated Royal Court rave, the performance ends with the affective release of a fictional resolution that bears no relationship to reality, while the gap between them is brushed away. Indeed, Vyper *remains* excluded; his story *is* capitalised on for the entertainment of Royal Court audiences without any benefit for him; and his counter-cultural form *does* get introduced into the gilded auditorium by someone more privileged than the community it emerged from. All the metatheatrical accusations Stevenson hurls at herself, in other words, remain valid. And yet, the fictional act of handing Vyper a microphone, ceding the stage, and allowing him to tell his story and the story of grime results in a de facto celebration of the inclusive power of theatre: a vehicle of social mobility that has worked for Stevenson, whose gain in cultural capital is patent on stage, but less so for (the real) Vyper, whose inclusion can happen only in fiction. The reality of his exclusion, however, is left affectively by the wayside.

Despite the many differences in tone, by turning the Royal Court into a grime rave, the play offers its spectators a similar invitation to that received by its Schaubühne counterparts. Through an ostensible reflection on exclusion, overshadowed by an individual, factual success story, and coupled with an unproblematised fictional one, *Poet in da Corner* gives rise to a feel-good celebration of its immediate cultural context. This testifies in turn to both the progressive role of theatre and its liberal audience's inclusive worldview, as they get up and dance to a formerly counter-cultural genre that has been subsumed into the market, and thus purged of its antagonistic force.[48]

For all the progressive politics embedded in them, what this section's case studies relay are stories of individual inclusion, through a mixture of talent and determination, modelling ways in which structural disadvantage, marginalisation, and trauma *can* be overcome through singular resilience – if only by some: those present to tell them, testifying to this possibility through the authenticity of the material, and normalising the individual nature of this uplift. In the collective celebration of stories of inclusion through theatre, embedded in

---

[48] Sharing grime music on YouTube was considered a 'key indicator of gang affiliation' by the Gang Matrix, a surveillance tool created by London's Metropolitan police and discontinued in February 2024 (Yeung, 2019).

their respective contexts, two different idealised notions of (certain types of) state-subsidised theatre emerge: in the UK, the nimble, business-savvy institution able to scout out Britain's untapped talent and capitalise on it for everyone's benefit, social and commercial at once; in Germany, the institutional node in a network of (mainly highbrow) cultural services for the citizen – a place in which uplift through traditional forms of education finds its embodied culmination. Both endure in a world in which the post-war promise of social mobility has fallen flat: indeed, 'the literary boom' of autofictional social mobility stories 'commenced when the economic one petered out' (Twellmann & Lammers, 2023: 51).[49] In this context, the absence from the theatre space of those who have not gone down this social mobility path – resolved on stage through various forms of fictionalised representation – tells its own, silent story, illustrating Louis's poignant definition of (bourgeois) culture as 'the gap between the people who have access to it and the people who don't'.[50]

5 Conclusion

This Element has considered a selection of plays produced by mainstage, state-subsidised venues in the larger cities of Britain and Europe to identify a theatrical mode that, while not radically new, is being deployed – as I have argued – in new ways and with new connotations. Rooted in lived experience, its oscillation between fact and fiction in negotiating the confines between selfhood and otherness, while performing the logics of social and political inclusion/exclusion, makes it 'zeitgeisty' in more ways than one. New is not only its resonance, in the hyper-narrative, post-truth communication economy – of which it shares the language and ambiguity, making it a privileged tool for both complicity and critique – but also its systematic naming and framing *as* autofiction. Originating in literary studies and then gradually applied to other fields, the autofictional as a label and analytic framework has yet to reach theatre studies, despite the mode's runaway and evidently transmedial popularity. Its advantages are manifold: as a framework, the autofictional helps nuance the analysis of theatrical works based on autobiographical material, shifting attention from their truth content to the choices – aesthetic, dramaturgical, and ethico-political – made in fictionalising the real. As this Element has demonstrated, it deals not in intrinsic properties, by asking what a work *is*, but in local, relational effects, probing what a work *does*.

---

[49] The same is true of New Labour's promise of a more inclusive society, as proven by recent data on the creative industries in general (see Comunian et al., 2023) and the performing arts in particular (see Friedman, O'Brien & Laurison, 2017).

[50] See footnote 43 (38:28).

By 'finding' a range of productions that function autofictionally, this Element has examined them – as Zwartjes suggests – 'alongside other conceptually-similar work', to identify the autofictional on stage and 'think about and probe the edges of that category, its functions and its politics, what new things it might offer us'. This has facilitated the singling out of three conceptual nodes, in the negotiation of which the political projects undergirding theatres of autofiction are at their most legible. Where relevant, this Element has referred not to autofictional theatre or drama but to theatres of autofiction, to emphasise the mode's localised, interactive, context-dependent, and shifting qualities: less an inherent property than a 'latent force' (Wagner-Egelhaaf, 2022: 26) to be scrutinised in practice, not defined in the abstract. As much as possible, it has gestured beyond the stage to society's metaphorical theatres of autofiction, to avoid an idealising isolation of theatrical production – a constant temptation for those invested in the medium and its possibilities – with an eye, instead, on theatre's place within cultural processes at large.

Iversen (2020: 561) identifies two takes on, or types of, autofiction: autofictional works can be seen either, in the wake of Doubrovsky, 'as poststructuralist or postmodern, as moves into or towards states of complete textualization such as that of the ultimate eradication of the self'; or, 'within a post-poststructuralist tendency, as a post-postmodernist text-type, intent on moving beyond the text towards the real'. It is this latter impetus – I have shown – that is dominant in theatres of autofiction. With one foot in the authenticity economy, playwrights fictionalising their lived experience tend to move from the real to the textual (broadly understood), and from the textual back to the real, with real-world, political struggles explicitly underpinning their self-fictionalising acts. Paradoxically, it is at its most textualised and self-aware – in plays like *Misty* or *salt.* – that the mode is at its most effective, its resistance to co-option most vigorous. It is when they successfully speak the language of the social-mediatised authenticity economy, in other words, valid-ating their place on stage, only to turn that language and its economy of value against itself that theatres of autofiction hold the most critical potential. Along the way, however, are a multitude of pitfalls, some of which are identified in this Element's analyses. On the tightrope between making work with a desire for it to 'shed its scare quotes' (Lerner, 2011: 101) and navigating the hypocrisies and risk of co-option therein; between breaking out of representational conventions mismatched with reality, and offering oneself up for consumption; between opening the self up to be both individual and collective, and speaking *for* or *as*; and between 'carrying the pain of others' (Louis & Taïa, 2018) and using them fictionally for one's own gain, theatres of autofiction shed light on the precarity and paradoxes of politicised culture today.

References

Ahmed, S. (2012). *On Being Included: Racism and Diversity in Institutional Life*. Chapel Hill, NC: Duke University Press.

Akbar, A. (2022). *The Corn Is Green Review – An Inspirational Heart-Warmer in Praise of Good Education*. www.theguardian.com/stage/2022/apr/24/the-corn-is-green-review-national-theatre-emlyn-williams.

AlJazeera English. *Studio B, Unscripted: With Ken Loach and Edouard Louis*. https://www.youtube.com/watch?v=J89RTrx1_eM.

Alter, A. & Harris, E. (2023). *Prince Harry's Memoir Has Record-Breaking Sales*. www.nytimes.com/2023/01/11/books/harry-memoir-sales-spare.html#:~:text=%E2%80%9CSpare%E2%80%9D%20sold%20more%20than%201.43,House%2C%20the%20world's%20largest%20publisher.

Angel-Perez, E., Rousseau, A. & Ayache, S. (2023). Feeling a Responsibility to Art: An Interview with Ella Hickson. In E. Angel-Perez and A. Rousseau, eds., *The New Wave of British Women Playwrights: 2008–2021*. Berlin: De Gruyter, pp. 227–238.

Angel-Perez, E. (2016). Écrire après la mort du théâtre: le théâtre post-post-dramatique de Tim Crouch et la scène anglaise contemporaine (UK). In C. Batlle, E. Gallén and M. Güell, eds., *Drame contemporain: renaissance ou extinction?*. Maó: Punctum, pp. 437–453.

Angel-Perez, E. (2013). Back to Verbal Theatre: Post-Post-Dramatic Theatres from Crimp to Crouch. *Études Britanniques Contemporaines*, 45. http://journals.openedition.org/ebc/862.

Behrendt, B. (2018). *Sex, Brutalität und der Kampf um die Deutungsmacht*. www.deutschlandfunkkultur.de/schaubuehne-berlin-im-herzen-der-gewalt-sex-brutalitaet-und-100.html.

Beswick, K. & Murray, C. (2022). *Making Hip Hop Theatre: Beatbox and Elements*. London: Methuen.

Beswick, K. (2020). Slaggy Mums: Class, Single Motherhood, and Performing Endurance. *Key Words: A Journal of Cultural Materialism*, 18, 94–113.

Beswick, K. (2014). Bola Agbaje's *Off the Endz*: Authentic Voices, Representing the Council Estate: Politics, Authorship and the Ethics of Representation. *Journal of Contemporary Drama in English*, 2(1), 97–112.

Blommaert, J., Smits, L. & Yacoubi, N. (2020). Context and its Complications. In A. De Fina, and A. Georgakopoulou, eds., *The CUP Handbook of Discourse Studies*. Cambridge: Cambridge University Press, pp. 52–69.

Bönisch, P. M. & Ostermeier, T. (2016). *The Theatre of Thomas Ostermeier*. Abingdon: Routledge.

Brouillette, S. (2020). *Sally Rooney's Couple Form.* https://post45.org/2020/06/sally-rooneys-couple-form/.

Carraway, C. (2018). *Refuge Woman.* Self-published zine.

Clark, A. (2018). *Drawn From Life: Why Have Novelists Stopped Making Things Up?* www.theguardian.com/books/2018/jun/23/drawn-from-life-why-have-novelists-stopped-making-things-up.

Comunian, R., Dent, T., O'Brien, D., Read, T. & Wreyford, N. (2023). *Making the Creative Majority: A report for the All-Party Parliamentary Group for Creative Diversity on 'What Works' to Support Diversity and Inclusion in Creative Education and the Talent Pipeline, with a Focus on the 16+ Age Category.* www.cultural/cultural/projects/creative-majority-education.

Crompton, S. (2023). *Interview. Playwright Alexander Zeldin: 'Lots of People Can Make a Living Being an Artist in France. In the UK, That's not the Case'.* www.theguardian.com/stage/2023/oct/15/alexander-zeldin-playwright-confessions-national-theatre-inequalities-trilogy-interview.

Dix, H. (2018). Introduction: Autofiction in English: The Story so Far. In H. Dix, ed., *Autofiction in English*, Cham: Palgrave Macmillan, pp. 1–23.

Doubrovsky, S. (2013). Autofiction. *Auto/Fiction* 1(1), 1–5.

Doubrovsky, S. (1993). Textes en Main. In S. Doubrovsky, J. Lecarme and P. Lejeune, eds., *Autofiction & Cie*, Nanterre: Université Paris X, pp. 207–217.

Edy, D. (2020). Transfuge(s) de classe, de genre, de culture... Pour Thomas Ostermeier, tous les détours mènent à Reims. In E. Kargl, & B. Terrisse, eds., *lendemains*, 45(180), 92–104.

Effe, A. & Lawlor, H. (2022). Introduction: From Autofiction to the Autofictional. In A. Effe and H. Lawlor, eds., *The Autofictional: Approaches, Affordances, Forms.* Cham: Palgrave Macmillan, pp. 1–18.

Ernaux, A. (2019). *Towards a Transpersonal 'I'.* Translated by D. M. Cornelio. www.annie-ernaux.org/texts/vers-un-je-transpersonnel-2/.

Ernaux, A. (2003). *L'Écriture comme un couteau: Entretien avec Frédéric-Yves Jeannet.* Paris: Gallimard.

Evans, D. (2023). *A Nation of Shopkeepers: The Unstoppable Rise of the Petty Bourgeoisie.* London: Repeater Books.

Felski, R. (2000). Nothing to Declare: Identity, Shame, and the Lower Middle Class. *PMLA*, 115(1), 33–45.

Fernandes, S. (2017). *Curated Stories: The Uses and Misuses of Storytelling.* Oxford: Oxford University Press.

Ferreira-Meyers, K. (2018). Does Autofiction Belong to French or Francophone Authors and Readers Only? In H. Dix, ed., *Autofiction in English*, Cham: Palgrave Macmillan, pp. 27–48.

Fischer-Lichte, E. (2014). *The Routledge Introduction to Theatre and Performance Studies*. Abingdon: Routledge.

Fix, F. and Toudoire-Surlapierre, F. eds. (2011). *L'autofiguration dans le théâtre contemporain: Se dire sur la scène*. Dijon: Editions Universitaires de Dijon.

Folarin, T. (2020). *Can a Black Novelist Write Autofiction?* https://newrepublic.com/article/159951/can-black-novelist-write-autofiction.

Friedman, S., O'Brien, D., & Laurison, D. (2017). 'Like Skydiving without a Parachute': How Class Origin Shapes Occupational Trajectories in British Acting. *Sociology*, 51(5), 992–1010.

Fournier, L. (2022). *Autotheory as Feminist Practice in Art, Writing, and Criticism*. Cambridge, MA: MIT Press.

Garvey, J. (2019). *Woman's Hour*. www.bbc.co.uk/sounds/play/m0002bms.

Genette, G. (1997). *Paratexts: Thresholds of Interpretation*. Translated by J. E. Lewin. New York: Cambridge University Press.

Genette, G. (1988). *Narrative Discourse Revisited*. Translated by J. E. Lewin. Ithaca, NY: Cornell University Press.

Georgakopoulou, A. (2022). Co-opting Small Stories on Social Media: A Narrative Analysis of the Directive of Authenticity. *Poetics Today*, 43(2), 265–286.

Gibbons, A. (2017). Contemporary Autofiction and Metamodern Affect. In R. van den Akker, A. Gibbons and T. Vermeulen, eds., *Metamodernism: Historicity, Affect, and Depth after Postmodernism*. London: Rowman and Littlefield, pp. 117–130.

Goodling, E. & Mark, L. (2022). 'Be Yourself, Inasmuch as it Suits the Job': 'Authenticity' at Berlin's Maxim Gorki Theater and London's Royal Court Theatre. *Comparative Drama*, 55(2), 39–66.

Haydon, A. (2017). *Home Strange Home*. www.nachtkritik.de/nachtkritiken/deutschland/berlin-brandenburg/berlin/schaubuehne-berlin/returning-to-reims-thomas-ostermeier.

Heddon, D. (2008). *Autobiography and Performance*. Basingstoke: Palgrave Macmillan.

Heddon, D. (2002). Performing the Self: Post-script. *M/C Journal*, 5(5). https://journal.media-culture.org.au/mcjournal/article/view/1982.

Hickson, E. (2018). *The Writer*. London: Nick Hern Books.

Hiden, R. (2020). Das Theater als For(u)m der Darstellung soziologischer Erkenntnisse: Didier Eribons Autosozioanalyse als künstlerisches Reenactment? In E. Kargl, & B. Terrisse, eds., *lendemains*, 45(180), 105–117.

Hill-Paul, L. (2022). *Mood on BBC Three: Showrunner Nicôle Lecky 'Didn't Identify' with Sasha 'It's Not Me'*. www.express.co.uk/showbiz/tv-radio/1573861/Mood-Nicole-Lecky-Sasha-identify-BBC-Three.

Hoggart, R. (1957). *The Uses of Literacy: Aspects of Working-Class Life*. London: Chatto and Windus.

Inchley, M. (2015). *Voice and New Writing, 1997-2007: Articulating the Demos*. Basingstoke: Palgrave Macmillan.

Iversen, S. (2020). Transgressive Narration: The Case of Autofiction. In M. Fludernik and M.-L. Ryan, eds., *Narrative Factuality*. Berlin: De Gruyter, pp. 555–563.

Jaffe, A. (2011). Sociolinguistic Diversity on Mainstream Media: Authenticity, Authority and Processes of Mediation and Mediatization. *Journal of Language and Politics*, 10, 562–586.

James, A. (2022). The Fictional in Autofiction. In A. Effe and H. Lawlor, eds., *The Autofictional: Approaches, Affordances, Forms*. Cham: Palgrave Macmillan, pp. 41–60.

Kargl, E. & Terrisse B. (2020). Editorial. *lendemains*, 45(180), 3–4.

Kellaway, K. (2014). *Rachel Cusk: 'Aftermath was Creative Death. I Was Heading into Total Silence.'* www.theguardian.com/books/2014/aug/24/rachel-cusk-interview-aftermath-outline.

Kelly, H. (2019). *Nicole Lecky Talks About Her Debut Play Opening at Royal Court Theatre That Explores Female Empowerment*. www.swlondoner.co.uk/nicole-lecky-interview/.

Kene, A. (2018). *Misty*. London: Nick Hern Books.

Knausgaard, K. O. (2016). *Karl Ove Knausgaard: The Shame of Writing about Myself*. www.theguardian.com/books/2016/feb/26/karl-ove-knausgaard-the-shame-of-writing-about-myself.

Kornbluh, A. (2023). *Immediacy, or the Style of Too Late Capitalism*. London: Verso.

Korthals Altes, L. (2014). *Ethos and Narrative Interpretation: The Negotiation of Values in Fiction*. Lincoln: University of Nebraska Press.

Lawless, J. (2023). *Prince Harry Says Explosive Book is a Bid to 'Own My Story'*. https://apnews.com/article/entertainment-united-kingdom-prince-harry-books-and-literature-nonfiction-7082bf624e4b43826d0cc39ce69f961f.

Lecky, N. (2019). *Superhoe*. London: Nick Hern Books.

Lejeune, P. (1975). *Le pacte autobiographique*, Paris: Éditions du Seuil.

Lerner, B. (2011). *Leaving the Atocha Station*. London: Granta.

Leroux, L.-P. (2004). Théâtre autobiographique : quelques notions. *Jeu* (111), 75–85.

Louis, E. (2018). *History of Violence*. Translated by L. Stein. New York: Farrar, Straus and Giroux.

Louis, E. & Taïa, A. (2018). *We Speak about Violence: Abdellah Taïa and Édouard Louis in Conversation*. www.theparisreview.org/blog/2018/07/02/we-speak-about-violence-abdellah-taia-and-edouard-louis-in-conversation/.

Marcus, L. (2022). Autofiction and Photography: 'The Split of the Mirror'. In A. Effe and H. Lawlor, eds., *The Autofictional: Approaches, Affordances, Forms*. Cham: Palgrave Macmillan, pp. 309–326.

Mark, L. (2023). 'Who Gets to Speak and How?': Staging Autofiction in Debris Stevenson's *Poet in da Corner* (2018) and Ella Hickson's *The Writer* (2018). In E. Angel-Perez and A. Rousseau, eds., *The New Wave of British Women Playwrights: 2008-2021*. Berlin: De Gruyter, pp. 131–150.

McClenaghan, M. (2018). *Refuge Woman: Live Journalism Experiment Reached New Audiences*. www.thebureauinvestigates.com/blog/2018-12-17/refuge-woman-the-live-journalism-experiment-that-changed-our-reporting.

Mead, R. (2014). *The Scourge of 'Relatability'*. www.newyorker.com/culture/cultural-comment/scourge-relatability.

Mäkelä, M. & Meretoja, H. (2022). Critical Approaches to the Storytelling Boom. *Poetics Today*, 43(2), 191–218.

Murray, C. (2019). Conrad Murray Artist Q&A at Tom Thumb Theatre. Online video clip. www.conradmurray.org/new-page.

Murray, C. (2022). DenMarked. In K. Beswick and C. Murray, eds., *Beats and Elements: A Hip Hop Theatre Trilogy*. London: Methuen, pp. 45–78.

Pavis, P. (2016). *The Routledge Dictionary of Performance and Contemporary Theatre*. Translated by A. Brown. Abingdon: Routledge.

Piketty, T. (2018). Brahmin Left vs Merchant Right: Rising Inequality and the Changing Structure of Political Conflict (Evidence from France, Britain and the US, 1948–2017). *WID.world*. http://piketty.pse.ens.fr/files/Piketty2018.pdf.

Przulj, T. (2022). Dialogic Reading Spaces in Autofiction: Rachel Cusk's Kudos. *Life Writing*, 20(2), 273–285.

Rebellato, D. (2009). When We Talk of Horses: Or, What Do We See When We See a Play? *Performance Research*, 14(1), 17–28.

Ricœur, P. (1999). Memory and Forgetting. In R. Kearney & M. Dooley, eds., *Questioning Ethics: Contemporary Debates in Philosophy*. London: Routledge, pp. 5–11.

Ricœur, P. (1990). *Time and Narrative Volume 3*. Translated by K. Blamey and D. Pellauer. Chicago, IL: The University of Chicago Press.

Satin, L. & Jerome, J. (1999). Introduction. *Women & Performance: A Journal of Feminist Theory*, 10(1–2), 9–19.

Schaeffer, J.-M. (2010). *Why Fiction?* Lincoln, NE: University of Nebraska Press.

Schmitt, A. (2022). The Pragmatics of Autofiction. In A. Effe and H. Lawlor, eds., *The Autofictional: Approaches, Affordances, Forms*. Cham: Palgrave Macmillan, pp. 83–100.

Schmitt, A. (2010). Making the Case for Self-Narration. Against Autofiction. *a/b. Auto/Biography Studies*, 25(1), 122–137.

Schulze, D. (2017). *Authenticity in Contemporary Theatre and Performance: Making it Real*. London: Methuen.

Smith, S. & Watson, J. (2001). *Reading Autobiography: A Guide for Interpreting Life Narratives*. Minnesota, MN: University of Minnesota Press.

Srikanth, S. (2019). Fictionality and Autofiction. *Style*, 63(3), 344–363.

Stephens, S. (2012). *Deutsch Courage: Why German Theatre Dares – And Wins*. www.theguardian.com/stage/theatreblog/2012/may/09/german-the atre-dares-three-kingdoms.

Stephenson, J. (2013). *Performing Autobiography: Contemporary Canadian Drama*. Toronto: University of Toronto Press.

Swift, A. (2020). *What's Fair About That?* www.lrb.co.uk/the-paper/v42/n02/ adam-swift/what-s-fair-about-that.

Taylor, B. (2021). *The Tiny White People in Our Heads: Black Subjectivity, Elaine De Kooning, Autofiction*. https://blgtylr.substack.com/p/the-tiny-white-people-in-our-heads.

Thompson, S. (2018). *salt*. London: Faber & Faber.

Thomson, G. A. (2018). More Life: On Contemporary Autofiction and the Scourge of Relatability. *Michigan Quarterly Review Online*. https://sites .lsa.umich.edu/mqr/2018/08/more-life-on-contemporary-autofiction-and-the-scourge-of-relatability/.

Tomlin, L. (2019). *Political Dramaturgies and Theatre Spectatorship: Provocations for Change*. London: Methuen.

Twellmann, M. & Lammers, P. (2023). Autosociobiography: A Travelling Form. *Comparative Critical Studies*, 20(1), 47–68.

van der Erve, L., Krutikova, S., Macmillan, L. & Sturrock, D. (2023). 'Intergenerational mobility in the UK'. *IFS Deaton Review of Inequalities*. https://ifs.org.uk/inequality/intergenerational-mobility-in-the-uk.

Wagner-Egelhaaf, M. ed. (2019). *Handbook of Autobiography/Autofiction*. Berlin: De Gruyter.

Wagner-Egelhaaf, Martina. (2022). Of Strange Loops and Real Effects: Five Theses on Autofiction/the Autofictional. In A. Effe and H. Lawlor, eds., *The Autofictional: Approaches, Affordances, Forms*. Cham: Palgrave Macmillan, pp. 21–40.

Weigel, P. (2011). Autofictions au théâtre : la demi-masque et la plume. In F. Fix and F. Toudoire-Surlapierre, eds., *L'autofiguration dans le théâtre contemporain: Se dire sur la scène*. Dijon: Editions Universitaires de Dijon, pp. 15–29.

White, G. (2013). *Audience Participation in Theatre: Aesthetics of the Invitation*. Basingstoke: Palgrave Macmillan.

Worthen, J. R. (2021). *Autofiction and Selfie Aesthetics*. https://post45.org/2021/12/autofiction-and-selfie-aesthetics/.

Yeung, P. (2019). *The Grim Reality of Life under Gangs Matrix, London's Controversial Predictive Policing Tool*. www.wired.co.uk/article/gangs-matrix-violence-london-predictive-policing.

Zarin, C. (2018). '*Returning to Reims': A German Theatre Company's Meditation on the Politics of Working-Class Families*. www.newyorker.com/culture/culture-desk/returning-to-reims-a-german-theatre-companys-meditation-on-the-politics-of-working-class-families.

Zipfel, F. (2014). Fiction across Media: Toward a Transmedial Concept of Fictionality. In M. L. Ryan and J.-N. Thön, eds., *Storyworlds across Media: Towards a Media-Conscious Narratology*. Lincoln, NE: University of Nebraska Press, pp. 103–125.

Zipfel, F. (2005). Autofiction. In D. Herman, M. Jahn, and M.-L. Ryan, eds., *Routledge Encyclopedia of Narrative Theory*. New York: Routledge, pp. 36–37.

Zwartjes, A. (2019). Under the Skin: An Exploration of Autotheory. *Assay: A Journal of Nonfiction Studies*, 6(1). www.assayjournal.com/arianne-zwartjes8203-under-the-skin-an-exploration-of-autotheory-61.html.

Acknowledgements

I wish to thank the Schaubühne, Katharina Langels, the Maxim Gorki Theater, the Berliner Ensemble, the Théâtre de Liège, and the Théâtre de l'Odéon for sharing production recordings with me, and to acknowledge with thanks the permission of Rich Lakos, Manuel Harlan, David Baltzer, Jean-Louis Fernandez, and Arno Declair to reproduce images. Parts of this project were developed during a fellowship at the Cluster of Excellence Temporal Communities: Doing Literature in a Global Perspective (EXC 2020), funded by the Deutsche Forschungsgemeinschaft (DFG, German Research Foundation) under Germany's Excellence Strategy. I am grateful to Ingo Berensmeyer, Michael Gamper, Jutta Müller-Tamm, Maraike Di Domenica, Raphaela Lösen, Annette Keck, and the LMU Mentorship Programme for the support and resources made available to me at Freie Universität Berlin and at Ludwig-Maximilians-Universität München. For their invaluable feedback on early drafts of this Element, my thanks go to Clio Unger, Peer Illner, Sean Mark, and Jacqueline Bolton. Heartfelt thanks also to the series editors, Liz Tomlin and Trish Reid, for their enduring generosity and mentorship, and to the anonymous reviewers for engaging so thoughtfully with my manuscript. I am grateful to many friends, colleagues, and mentors for their input at various stages of the research project this Element is part of: among them, Alan Read, Siân Adiseshiah, Maggie Inchley, Louise Owen, Mark Currie, Ingo Berensmeyer, Gero Guttzeit, Daniel Schneider, Sonja Trurnit, Torsten Jost, Alexandra Ksenofontova, Till Kadritzke, Raphaëlle Efoui-Delplanque, Alix Ricau, Sophia Brown, Nicholas Holden, Emily Goodling, Sabine Erbrich, and Henry Ravenhall. Special thanks to Katie Beswick for her kindness in sharing suggestions and writing with me. Finally, for their enduring support, thanks to my friends, brothers, and parents, and – as always, for everything – to Peer.

Cambridge Elements ☰

Theatre, Performance and the Political

Trish Reid
University of Reading

Trish Reid is Professor of Theatre and Performance and Head of the School of Arts and Communication Design at the University of Reading. She is the author of *The Theatre of Anthony Neilson* (2017), *Theatre & Scotland* (2013), *Theatre and Performance in Contemporary Scotland* (2024) and co-editor of the *Routledge Companion to Twentieth-Century British Theatre* (2024).

Liz Tomlin
University of Glasgow

Liz Tomlin is Professor of Theatre and Performance at the University of Glasgow. Monographs include *Acts and Apparitions: Discourses on the Real in Performance Practice and Theory* (2013) and *Political Dramaturgies and Theatre Spectatorship: Provocations for Change* (2019). She edited *British Theatre Companies 1995–2014* (2015) and was the writer and co-director with Point Blank Theatre from 1999–2009.

About the Series

Elements in Theatre, Performance and the Political showcases ground-breaking research that responds urgently and critically to the defining political concerns, and approaches, of our time. International in scope, the series engages with diverse performance histories and intellectual traditions, contesting established histories and providing new critical perspectives.

Cambridge Elements ⁼

Theatre, Performance and the Political

Printed in the United States
by Baker & Taylor Publisher Services